The Deacon Letters
From a Montana Woman to Her Church Family

1995 - 2005

by Caroline Conklin

Illustrated by Kathleen Petersen

PRESS

For Laverne

Index of Letters

Introduction
The Deacon Letters: From a Montana Woman to Her Church Family

These letters were written over ten of my fifteen years as an ordained Vocational Deacon in the Diocese of Montana, at the Church of the Incarnation in Great Falls, Montana. Most were printed in the monthly church bulletin, "The Messenger." I am greatly indebted to the editor of that publication, Vi Stahlecker, for her expertise, assistance and encouragement.

I wrote the Letters from three perspectives: one vast, one confined, and one walled yet infinite.

Great Falls lies in the windy Montana plains, country of the Big Sky. The perspective is large, subtly colored in shades of yellow and brown, green and blue. The city's population of around 60,000 has stayed much the same over the years. People come and go, but the view from the town of the earth and the heavens is essentially changeless and unforgettable.

My second and smaller perspective was from a brown split-level house at the edge of town. After retiring in 1995 from a 24-year career as a Speech/ Language Pathologist for the Great Falls School District, I spent much of my time within that house. I took delight in living there, not only for the views of the Little Belt Mountains to the south and the open field to the west, not only for Bill my husband who shared the house with me, for our grown children Sarah, Matthew and Mary, for our companion animals, but for the rooms and the objects in those rooms.

To explain the importance of my third perspective, the view from inside the church, I must tell you my story:

My husband Bill and I met as students at Harvard/ Radcliffe and married in 1958. Two children were born to us: Sarah in 1965 and Tom in 1967. Tom drowned at the age of 3 when the car in which he was riding went into the Blackfoot River. Two years later, Bill and I adopted a brother and sister, Mary age 3, and Matthew age 18 months.

Twenty years after Tom's death, following many years of service as a lay person, I was asked by the Diocese to consider becoming a Vocational Deacon. It felt right. On June 24, 1991, after two years of training in the scripture, history, practicalities and discipline of the church, and a summer of Clinical Pastoral Education as a hospital chaplain in Spokane, I became an ordained person. After that I entered in a new way my home church, the Church of the Incarnation, a lovely Gothic stone building with stained glass windows and a high arched ceiling. From within that church, I engaged in the liturgy, counseled, preached, taught and prayed with my church family. No Big Sky is visible from inside there, no mountains or fields, only the vastness of eternity.

Sarah now lives in Seattle, where Bill and I live too, and Mary lives in Montana. Both daughters are leading happy, productive lives. Matthew, however, suffered from bad luck and life-long depression. In 2003, at the age of 32, estranged from his wife and while Bill and I were out of town, Matthew took his own life through a combination of pills and carbon monoxide from the vehicles in our garage.

I know that the deaths of children are nearly as hard to read about as they are to tell. But what happened, happened. After the deaths of both of our sons I turned in my grief to God, family, friends, and church. I'm still doing that.

Soon after retiring from the active Diaconate in 2005, I began readying these letters for publication. I am eternally grateful to my cousin Kathleen Petersen who has enhanced them immeasurably with her illustrations.

I believe that even though life is difficult and often tragic, we may be sustained by many things:

By thanking God.
By asking God for the strength to do what's
right.
By living into the day-to-day moments of our
lives.
By using fully our God-given abilities.
By cherishing family and friends.

*By striving to include, help, and learn from the
    stranger.
By choosing cheerfulness over gloom.*

My hope is that these glimpses from my life's journey will be helpful to you as you travel your own.

Caroline Conklin (The Reverend)
Seattle, Washington
March 2007

One

Clink!

August 1995

Dearly beloved: We have come together in the presence of God to witness and bless the joining together of this man and this woman in Holy Matrimony.
- *The Book of Common Prayer, p. 423*

On August 23rd, Bill and I will have a restaurant dinner with wine to celebrate the 37th anniversary of our wedding, which took place at St. John's Episcopal Church, in Crawfordsville, Indiana. I wore a princess-style white satin gown my mother had made. My sisters, Jean Katharine in blue and Harriet Edith in pink, were my bridesmaids. After the ceremony, we set out in a squat black '50 Chevy on a wedding trip that would eventually take us to Missoula, where Bill would start his second year of law school. On the way, we would honeymoon at Banff and Lake Louise.

I carried some smelly cheese in the glove compartment that made Bill feel sick. He led me on a long mountain hike that made me feel sick. We both wondered what we were getting into. We still wonder, and are still willing to keep trying to find out.

We've experienced intense joy from one another and from our children, and almost insupportable grief when our three-year-old son Tom drowned in an accident in 1971. Somehow we keep going. God knows we've done our best and God knows we've made mistakes. In many ways we've been lucky. We've had our health and sufficient income, and we live at a time and in a place relatively free from war, pestilence and persecution.

It has helped that we married young, came from similar backgrounds, and held similar political beliefs. If we'd taken one of the compatibility tests currently used by churches to prepare engaged couples for marriage, we probably would have scored high. Instead, we were counseled by a priest, and though neither of us remembers what he told us, I'm sure his counsel was wise.

There's much to be said for the shared history, the support and comfort that a long relationship can give. A conversation begun on the day a couple meets continues until the day they part forever. If that's not a miracle, it's at least something to wonder at.

By living in a lasting marriage and observing many others, as well as some that don't last, I've learned that the real family values are mutual affection, respect, and commitment. When one person in a family dominates and attempts to diminish the others, preventing them from fulfilling their own God-given promise and potential, then any other worthwhile values that family may exemplify will not be enough to redeem it.

I have also learned that many people find mutual affection, respect and commitment from long-term arrangements of friends and kinfolk that differ from the standard one of man-woman-child. God-filled families exist in many forms.

Here's a glass raised. Join us as we celebrate our years together. Perhaps you have such a celebration soon in your own life. Clink!

Thank You God for the long conversations of my life.

Two

Love's Labor

September 1995

But Martha was distracted by her many tasks; so she came to him and asked, "Lord, do you not care that my sister has left me to do all the work by myself? Tell her then to help me." But the Lord answered her, "Martha, Martha, you are worried and distracted by many things; there is need of only one thing. Mary has chosen the better part, which will not be taken away from her." - Luke 10:40-42

This Labor Day, for the first time in 24 years, the school doors will open and close without me. No desk or message box or District Directory will carry my name. Much of what has occupied my days I will never do again. It's an odd feeling. I went to the dictionary to see if Labor Day is something a retired person can celebrate, and found that to labor is "to exert one's powers of body or mind." What a great definition! Nothing there about producing or succeeding or earning or taking over. To exert one's powers. So simple.

No matter our age or station, by asking God's guidance we can exert our powers in ways that express the complete person God intends us to be. After all, Jesus left his paid work and called others from theirs. The world may say we are too old or tired or weak or foolish to labor any longer, but we and God know better.

Mary of Bethany, taking time out from the work of the household, chose to sit by Jesus and learn. What do you suppose came of that choice? Maybe she wrote letters or a book now lost to us. Maybe people sat at her feet while she passed on her knowledge. Perhaps she wove God's glory into garments and bed covers, sowed it into flower and herb gardens. Possibly she passed along her unique wisdom simply by the way she ordered her days, laughed and talked with friends, conducted herself through her last illness.

Mary of Bethany knew in her heart that her choices for herself were God's choices. In Luke 10, she chose to listen to Jesus. In John 12, she asked no one's permission to anoint Jesus' feet with oil and dry them with her hair. While Jesus lived, she tended to and learned from him. When he died, she was forcibly retired from being his disciple and friend. She might have used that as an excuse to lose heart, to sit staring into space or go into an early decline. But I don't think she did. After Jesus' death, Mary's discipline had to come from within. For her, this would not be a problem. Like Jesus, she cared little for other people's opinions. She knew from where her inner voice came. The one thing we may be sure of about Mary's post-Jesus life is that she lived it her way, God's way. I think that she labored on in love of God, self and neighbor until she joined her Teacher in glory.

Strengthen me God to use my free hours to exert my powers for Your purposes.

Three

What Aunt Dorothy Taught
October 1995

Wisdom teaches her children
and gives help to those who seek her.
  - Sirach 4:11

My mother's parents, Clyde and Hattie Wylie, homesteaded in Idaho from Iowa early in this century. They raised five sons and three daughters. My mother's sister Dorothy, born in Burley in 1909, lived in Boise for much of her life. Widowed young, this shy, generous, wise woman worked for the government and raised her two children, Kathleen and Kermit, on her own.

This June, at the age of 86, she died of ovarian cancer in Kathleen's home, tended by her daughter, a hospice nurse, and me. Two months earlier, Kathleen had asked her mother what she wanted for her birthday. Characteristically, Dorothy said, "Nothing."

So Kathleen sat down and wrote out the things her mother had taught her over the years—taught her not so much by words as by her underlying philosophy and example. She presented the list to Dorothy, who was pleased and touched.

Here are <u>Mother's Instructions</u> by Kathleen Ragain Petersen:

1) Don't keep score. Help people when they need it. They'll never pay you back, they'll do better than that—they will pass it on.
2) Don't "post mortem." The future is more interesting than the past.
3) Don't complain; don't explain. People have their own problems. They'll only hear yours if it matches one of theirs.
4) Read everything. You'll never be bored, lonely or uninteresting if you can read.
5) Eat a balanced diet, and put butter on everything.
6) Always make the bed.
7) Don't leave home if the kitchen is messy.
8) Fix yourself up, but don't obsess about it.
9) Be fair; life isn't.
10) It's okay to be sad. Not everyone has to be happy all the time or in a good mood all the time. Just don't blame it on, or take it out on, anyone else when you're feeling bad.
11) Don't find fault with other people. They're probably doing the best they can.
12) Don't find fault with yourself. Fix what you can and forgive the rest.
13) Keep track of the government but don't let it drive you crazy.
14) Pay your bills.
15) Listen to music.
16) You don't have to show your poker hand unless someone has paid to see it.

Many good people leave such legacies as this. You know some. Let them know what they have taught you. There's no greater compliment.

Thank You God for those who have taught me over the years.

Four

Noticing Purple

November 1995

When they had gone ashore, they saw a charcoal fire there, with fish on it, and bread. Jesus said to them, "Bring some of the fish that you have just caught." So Simon Peter went aboard and hauled the net ashore, full of large fish, a hundred fifty-three of them; and though there were so many, the net was not torn. Jesus said to them, "Come and have breakfast." - John 21:9-12a

Jesus said it over and over, by story and by example. *You have so much! Only look and you will see.*

God's great abundance is never to be taken for granted. God sends not only wine for the wedding at Cana, but too much wine and of the best quality. Not only loaves of bread but baskets left over. Not only a welcome for the prodigal, but a fatted calf. In this Gospel story, Jesus, who has been crucified and is risen, returns to show the disciples where to fish. And so many fish! Soon he will share their breakfast, savoring with them God's surprising plenty.

A good way to appreciate God's abundance is to focus attention on a single part of it. Counting things like fish and wine jars is a way. So is seeing color. In her book <u>The Color Purple</u>, Alice Walker writes about her experiences growing up as a black woman in the deep South. A friend tells the narrator that God wants to share the beauties of creation with God's people. The friend says, *I think it pisses God off if you walk by the color purple in a field somewhere and don't notice it.*

Notice purple. See how very much there is in God's world! Try this. Take an imaginary paint pot full of God's glorious purple and splash it around the Biblical breakfast scene. Add a purple streak to the dawn. To the sun-lit peaks of the little waves, give a shifting purple tinge. Give that boat pale purple sails. On the shore, fill in a line of purple flowers where the sand meets the grass. Walk over to Jesus now. Purple the crackling flames close to the charcoal. Over his renewed body, chilled by the dawn breeze off the water, drape a warm wool purple cloak.

See how Jesus smiles.

I just walked through my house of twenty years, noticing purple. It made me smile. I saw with new eyes the purple hairbows in my portrait, painted by my Aunt Kiki when I was six. The purple cover on a Bible dictionary. The purple sheets on our bed. The purple oven mitt. The purple candle by my reading chair. Outside, the purple streaks of clouds just above the dawn lighting the Highwood Mountains.

Try walking through your own rooms, noticing God's purple. Warm yourself in it, as I did. You'll smile, too.

Thank You God for the rich colors of my life.

Five

Penny the Commonplace Penguin
December 1995

Very truly, I tell you, the one who believes in me will also do the works that I do and, in fact, will do greater works than these, because I am going to the Father. - John 14:12

Yesterday, for the first time this season, I heard the song, "Rudolph the Red-Nosed Reindeer." I turned off the radio.

It's not that I think Christmas sights and sounds come too soon, because I don't. I love the little colored lights and the Dickensian carolers and the Santas holding pop bottles. At least once a season, one of the familiar symbols sends me into weightless, timeless, untroubled childlike joy.

But not Rudolph. Of course he's cute as the dickens, serves others and turned a handicap into an asset. But I find it hard to identify with him. It's partly because he's unique—after all, only nine reindeer out of all the herds in Lapland fly, and only one has a luminous nose. It's partly because he was shunned for his odd appearance until noticed by the Front Office and then fawned over (so to speak). It's partly because he uses his special talent to deliver still more toys to already overburdened Western children.

In a recent <u>New Yorker</u> cartoon by S Gross, I saw what, to me, is a more admirable flying winter creature. I've named her Penny.

In the cartoon several penguins are standing on an iceberg with their little wings hanging down at their sides, looking up at a penguin who's soaring above them, little wings outspread. She's calling back down, "We just haven't been flapping them hard enough!"

How many penguins can fly? So far only the one, but they all have the means, however vestigial. Penny doesn't say, "Look at me! I can fly!" She says, "We." *We can all do it. We can go anywhere and do anything. We can be free.* And she tells them how.

Jesus brought us instructions for freedom from bondage, escape from exile. *Follow me,* he said. *Have faith and who knows what you can do.*

Jesus was once a human child. To be a young human means to be utterly helpless and then to discover amazing powers within oneself: the ability to grasp what is needed, the capacity to rise to one's feet and walk, the tools to speak. Maybe a sense of unlimited potential is the source of childhood joy. Young children aspire; their hopes soar. *I've come such a long way already. How much farther might I go?* Soon enough we start to fail at things, to fall back, to disappoint. Gradually we lower our personal expectations. Jesus knows that, from experience. And yet he says: *You can do as I do and more. Follow me.* Who are we to argue?

Strengthen me God to use fully the abilities You gave me.

Six

God at Four O'Clock

January 1996

The next day John was standing with two of his disciples, and as he watched Jesus walk by, he exclaimed, "Look, here is the Lamb of God!" The two disciples heard him say this, and they followed Jesus. When Jesus turned and saw them following, he said to them, "What are you looking for?" They said to him, "Rabbi, where are you staying?" He said to them, "Come and see." They came and saw where he was staying, and they remained with him that day. It was about four o'clock in the afternoon. - John 1:35-39

Some of us are morning people and some of us are evening people, but if there are four o'clock in the afternoon people, I've yet to meet one.

Four is definitely not a prime time for most of us. Four is when the scratchy throat turns sore, when the distance between us and our faraway loved ones stretches the longest. Four is when the slighting comment we overheard on Saturday stabs us as painfully as it did at the time. Four is when our failures stand out in bold print and our successes fade into illegibility. Four is when any ambitions we might have for our future seem useless.

Yet John the Baptist chose "about four o'clock in the afternoon" to reveal Jesus to his, John's, disciples as God's own child.

"What are you looking for?" Jesus asks, but the disciples don't answer. Probably they can't remember just then, it being the time it is. Instead they have the wit to ask, "Where are you staying?" (In case the answer occurs, they can get back to him.) Jesus says, "Come and see," and they turn and follow. It's as simple as that.

By the way, I wonder how they knew the time. Maybe someone who was there reported to the writer, "You know, it was that low time of day." Ah. Must have been about four o'clock.

After all, what better time than our lowest to turn from our own way (where were we headed after all) toward God? When our own plans seem least likely to succeed is the best time to remember that God's is the only Plan that will work. It's the best time to remember that God works through us, through you and me. We are not useless to God, at any time of day.

How do we move ourselves to a place where we can listen to God? Not everyone's way is the same. Maybe God speaks to you through another human, in person or in print. Maybe wordless music or utter silence brings you to God. Some of us meditate, saying a phrase over and over, or praying the Jesus prayer, or attending to the breath that moves through our bodies. Some of us find God when we work with our hands—with needle and thread, pencil and pad, with wood or glass or plants or bread dough. The way is less important than the intentionality.

At our own four o'clock in the afternoon, whenever that may happen, we simply need say, "I'm tired, I'm achy, I'm discouraged, God. Evening is coming on and tomorrow doesn't look much better. Where are you staying?"

See if God doesn't answer, "Come and see."

Thank You God for the vulnerable hours of my life when I am most ready for You.

Seven

Breaking the Ropes

February 1996

Accomplish in us the work of your salvation.
That we may show forth your glory in the world.
- The Book of Common Prayer p. 268

A 1939 full-length cartoon feature by Dave and Max Fleischer was "Gulliver's Travels." The scene I remember best is a huge Gulliver in Lilliput, flat on his back, surrounded by tiny humans and immobilized by hundreds of ropes that tied him down even by his hair.

At the age of four, though small, I could still identify with that Gulliver. Often I felt big and clumsy— because I was bigger than I had been, and growing. Too heavy to carry. Outdistancing my clothes. Able to do unintentional harm to fragile objects and small creatures. I hadn't yet come to terms with my size. It's hard to be big. It was hard then, and it's hard now.

It's especially hard to be as big as God intends us to be. Big in love. Big in works.

So we avoid standing up and stretching ourselves. We squander our time and energy on the habits that tie us down and immobilize us. We are Gulliver and we are the Lilliputians too, carelessly manufacturing the very ropes that bind us.

The ways we squander time and energy differ from person to person, but each of us knows our own. Television, alcohol, work, drugs, shopping—the list is endless. We know when we are binding ourselves. We also know when we are acting in ways that please God: when we are creating, or really listening to someone else, or walking slowly with a child, or volunteering at a mission, or opening a study-program book. It feels good. It feels, most of all, freeing.

Ash Wednesday is about the use and misuse of our lives. As Jesus spent 40 days in the wilderness apart from everything, so we can use that time to put away some binding habit. Then, rather than find another, we can turn our freedom over to God. Let's say that at the five o'clock hour we usually drink cocktails, or play golf or a computer game, or get in some after-hours work. This Lent, we can release that hour to gaze out the window, or to walk along the river, or meditate and pray. We can consciously and intentionally give that time over to God. We may find that God will make surprising use of it.

With God's grace, we can rip away those tough little ropes that limit our movement. Loosen a hand and flex our fingers. Kick free a foot and test the firm ground underneath. Gingerly release strands of hair. Lift ourselves up, look around, get a glimpse of the space God has reserved for us. Gasp as we sense what it might be to rise to our full height as God's child and stride freely through our lives.

Strengthen me God to loosen my binding habits.

Eight

All Things . . .

March 1996

All things bright and beautiful, all creatures great and small,
All things wise and wonderful, the Lord God made them all. – Hymnal #405 Words by Cecil Frances Alexander

Not long ago I was walking an Adopted section of highway with people from Bill's law office. Four times a year we walk that stretch, wearing orange vests and dragging black plastic bags to pick up trash.

I didn't much want to go this time, so I tried a useful attitude-adjustment device known as Conscious Gratitude. Walking along, I prayed silently. *Thank you God for sun and sky, for birds and cows, for waving knobbed grasses, for the nearby stubbled hayfield. Thank you God that I can walk without pain or exhaustion, that my eyes can see the trash and my hands pick it up. Thank you God for the human skills that made this road and the cars zooming by, as well as these cans and bottles and boxes and bags. Thank you for the nourishment most of these containers held—the hamburgers, pizzas, milk.*

Then I thought about the hymn "All things bright and beautiful." And then the Monty Python parody: "All things dull and ugly, All creatures short and squat. All things rude and nasty, the Lord God made the lot." Which of course is true, too. God not only made but loves these unattractive things. This is lucky for us, because if sinless slugs were not lovable to God, what chance would there be for you and me? Seldom do we manage to be either bright or beautiful, let alone both at once.

So my litany expanded: *Thank you God for the poisonous hiding snakes, for stinging clicking bugs, for creeping noxious weeds, for the unspeakable contents of this plastic bag, for the jerks who throw trash out car windows may they rot forever in...*

No, no. Somehow I'd lost the spirit of the thing. Anyway, are we so different? Maybe we ourselves don't litter. But each of us Americans generates a mountain of garbage in our lifetime. We throw away more nourishment than most people in the world ever see in their bowls. We use up many times more of the world's resources than anyone else does. We fill earth and sea with un-biodegradable substances that will still be around thousands of years after we are gone. We need to acknowledge that. We need to try to do something about it, and there are many resources that tell us how to lessen our personal damage to the Earth, and to help fix the root problems.

Cleaning a highway section can be a motivating experience, to say the least.

Strengthen me God to be a better steward of Your gifts.

Nine

God Gently Laughs

April 1996

Lay aside immaturity, and live,
and walk in the way of insight. - *Proverbs 9:6*

One theory about the origin of April Fools' Day is this: When the calendar was altered to begin the year in January rather than in the spring, some people refused to accept the change. They continued to live as though under the old system—New Years Day on April 1st—and were called April Fools because of it. These early Fools were afraid bad things would happen with a drastic calendar change like that. They couldn't see that the actual date of the new year was less important than was community consensus about it.

They were foolish to worry.

When it became clear that our daughter Sarah was going to be born on April 1st, I worried all the way to the then-brand-new Deaconess Hospital over how she might be teased. As it turned out, the date of her birth has been fun for her, and easy for family and friends to remember.

I was foolish to worry.

So what's wrong with being foolish? Nothing is wrong, unless we hang on to our misconceptions and act on them, and our actions work to the detriment of someone else. The more power we have, the more harmful our wrong-thinking. Because a foolish ruler can do great damage, Fools or Jesters were attached to royal courts from Egyptian times until the 18th century. Their role was to check and balance. They were allowed to speak unpopular truths without consequences, in order to prevent kings and queens from making bad mistakes. (Some say that the original truth-sayer in "The Emperor's New Clothes" was not a child, but a Court Fool.)

We don't have hired Fools to help us keep our perspective. We must recognize the simpleton in ourselves, and change our ideas when those ideas are proven wrong. It helps to believe that God smiles indulgently when we talk or act foolishly, and still loves us. Bolstered by God's steadfast love, we must think as clearly and wisely as we can, laugh when we get it wrong, and try to get it right.

Today let's look at ourselves in the mirror and make a silly face. Can we love a face like that? God can. Then let's bring to mind one of our prejudices and see if maybe condemning that particular thing or person or group of people makes no sense. Finally let's smile with God at our foolishness—and change.

Strengthen me God to rid myself of foolish, harmful misperceptions.

Ten

Mary's House

May 1996

When Jesus saw his mother and the disciple whom he loved standing beside her, he said to his mother, "Woman, here is your son." Then he said to the disciple, "Here is your mother." And from that hour the disciple took her into his own home." – John 19:26,27

This Easter Sunday afternoon 30 of us tourists, mostly Roman Catholics, took a bus to church from the cruise ship Star Odyssey docked near Kusadasi, Turkey. We traveled up a winding road overlooking the ruined but still beautiful Greco-Roman city of Ephesus. Our destination was a church service at Mary's House.

Turkey is 96% Muslim. The other 4% include Christians, most of whom are Eastern Orthodox and celebrate Easter on a different date. Yet Ephesus was not only home to one of the Christian communities founded by Paul, it is also home to a lovely tradition.

Many say that John was the Beloved Disciple to whom Jesus from the cross entrusted the care of his mother. Since John was later associated with Ephesus, it is also said that he brought her here. The vision of a 19th century German nun placed Mary in a certain small stone house, high above the city.

We were met by a contemporary nun, a young blue-habited American who was thrilled for us because we had the good luck to be in such a sacred place on such a day. She showed us through the house, a shrine lit and warmed by the wax tapers of supplicants burning before a small bronze statue of Mary.

For the service, we entered a small room, maybe 15 by 25 feet. The room was a study in contrasts. It had a black marble floor, white marble altar, scattering of lovely Turkish rugs, shiny communion silver, gold-cloth wall hangings, and wooden Byzantine-style crucifix. Yet all this opulence was set inside mud-colored walls with bare light bulbs in the ceiling, where we sat on folding chairs.

The priest was an elderly man from Malta with excellent English and a fine gold chasuble. Our missals were printed in eight languages. The priest gave a muddled but heart-felt sermon about his own bewilderment at being called to such a Christless place as Turkey, and about the sad state of Christianity today. At the end we sang, "Ave, Ave, Ave Maria." I wept a little at the beauty of it.

Outside, I looked down at the view Mary might have seen. It's a lovely spot, high in thickly wooded hills overlooking vineyards, olive groves, tobacco and wheat fields. Now, because of silt fill, one can barely glimpse the Aegean Sea. But Mary would have seen it. Ephesus at its peak was a port city.

When Paul arrived, Mary would have been in her seventies. (Did he meet her? If there's a tradition about that, I don't know it.) By then, many pilgrims must have walked or ridden donkeys and carts up to see this compassionate, God-centered, wise and innovative woman. She must have been a wonderful person, to have raised such a child as Jesus. I wish I could have been one of her visitors. Meanwhile it was awe-inspiring just to be stand where Mary herself might have stood.

Thank You God for Mary and all Your Saints.

Eleven

Nearer to Thee

June 1996

Nearer, my God, to Thee, nearer to Thee!
E'en though it be a cross that raiseth me,
Still all my song shall be, nearer, my God to Thee.

Refrain

Nearer my God to Thee,
Nearer to Thee! – Words by Sarah F. Adams, 1841

At Santorini, a lovely Greek island with cliff tops that appear snowy because of the white-washed houses, the harbor was too shallow for our cruise ship to dock. We had to anchor off shore and take tenders—motorized life boats—the rest of the way.

The sea was rough, the roughest we were to know it on this cruise. Our little boat was tossed high, first on one side then the other. Most of us got wet. People laughed, comparing the ride to something found at Disney World.

After a beautiful day on the island, we boarded the tenders to return to the ship. But though the sea was no rougher, we soon began to realize that we were marking time there on the waves as the mother ship, the Star Odyssey, moved away. The gap between her and us wasn't narrowing steadily, as we expected, but widening.

Because of the engine sounds of our little boat, the danger of getting up and moving around, and the language barrier between us and the Filipino crew, we couldn't find out what was going on. Instead we could only wait, uncertain and decidedly uncomfortable.

What was going on? Had we been forgotten, abandoned? Was the boat crew deserting? The ship hijacked? Undergoing a bomb search? Sinking? No one mentioned Disney World now, and the person who began singing "Nearer My God to Thee" (the song reportedly played as the Titanic went down) was quickly hushed.

I wondered how many of us felt nearer to God in those minutes of perceived danger. No way of knowing. I thought of Jesus in a small boat in the storm-tossed Sea of Galilee. He was sleeping in the back of the boat when the waves came up, and the panicky disciples woke him. He calmed the sea, then chided the men for lack of faith. (*Luke 8:22-25*) Jesus was always in the boat, but so long as things were going well, the disciples were asleep to him.

Ocean liners like the Titanic, and cruise ships like the Star Odyssey, are designed to resemble luxury hotels so that nervous passengers can pretend the ground is still solid beneath them. But sea is not land and, despite our hubris, no human enterprise is unsinkable.

As for our little boat, very soon it began moving toward the ship and we were back on board in time for the evening meal. They told us that the ship's anchor had been dragging so the captain raised it while he located a less sandy area of seat bottom. Only then could the tenders safely return.

We were never in true peril, not really. But the reminder of our perilous state in this life, our dependence on God who is always there, was a good thing. I'm grateful for the experience.

Thank You God for Your nearness to me in good times and bad.

Twelve

Riding in the Car

July 1996

Preserve those who travel; surround them with your loving care; protect them from every danger; and bring them in safety to their journey's end; through Jesus Christ our Lord. Amen. – The Book of Common Prayer, p. 831

In the summer of 1940, my college professor father received a Guggenheim research grant for his projected textbook <u>State Taxation of Metallic Deposits</u>. Our parents put my sister Jean Katharine, age 11, and me, age 5, in the back seat of the new gray Dodge and drove away from Cleveland, Ohio for a trip around the country. We sang "The Sunny Side of the Street," "Animal Fair" and "We're Off to See the Wizard."

We saw no wizards but we did visit the wonders of more than twenty states, including Montana, and Idaho where my mother's family lived.

Traveling wasn't easy then. We stayed in Tourist Cabins because the word "motel" for "motor hotel" hadn't been invented. The Tourist Cabins were likely to be buggy and none too clean. "Modern" on the sign meant indoor plumbing, though it took us an uncomfortable night or two to figure that out.

Cars were less reliable, too. Engines overheated. Tires went flat. Gas quality was uncertain. Roads were poorly maintained. Service stations were infrequent and highly individual. Perhaps you've seen the 1940 Edward Hopper painting called "Gas," showing a man standing by red gasoline pumps on a lonely, wooded roadway? That brings back memories!

We girls were fine. We had our toys and books, our imaginations, and a food supply in a wicker basket by Mother's feet. What did we care for gas or gas money, for maps or washed-out bridges, for breakdowns? We could see our parents and hear their voices, and so we were content.

Often since, I've wondered at our parents' courage in taking two small children on such a trip. In the same way I wonder at the courage we all show when we climb into a car and drive off, especially when so many of us have had a first-hand experience of injury and death in road accidents.

But then, what gives us the courage even to get up in the morning? To journey through our day and do what must be done? With God's help, we do our best to be productive and safe and loving. With God's assurance, we know that most of the time things go well. Good cheer, gratitude and hopefulness are traits we share as believers.

Many of us will be traveling by car this summer. Besides asking God that the engine run smoothly, we can be thankful for the hope and confidence that keep our hands on the wheel and our hearts filled with happiness.

Strengthen me God to keep alert when I drive the car.

Thirteen

The Guest Room Bed

August 1996

Do not neglect to show hospitality to strangers, for by doing that some have entertained angels without knowing it. – Hebrews 13:2

We've always welcomed company, and thought of ourselves as hospitable people. Over the years we've put up relatives, old friends, exchange students from Mexico and France, New Zealand visitors, stumping candidates, traveling clergy, and symphony guest artists.

For some of these years, they slept on a copper-colored pull-out sofa known as The Guest Room Bed.

Last year David, one of Sarah's friends, complained to her that the bed was uncomfortable, and she told us. "Huh," I sniffed to myself. "Ingrate. See if he's invited again."

But because of what David had said, Bill and I finally slept in the guest room bed, which is something we should have done the night it entered the house. Well, you guessed it. The bed was definitely uncomfortable. It had lumps, hard areas and sags. Finding a sleeping spot was not easy. Embarrassing? I guess! My first impulse was to write to everyone who'd slept there and apologize, but Bill's cooler head prevailed.

So to all the gracious people who never let on, who bravely said, "Oh yes, we slept just fine," we say "sorry" and "thanks."

With a special, grudging, thanks to David the truth-sayer.

Of course the bed may have been the least of our guests' problems with us. Asked later, any one of them might have said, "The bed? Not good, but I didn't mind that so much as I did their pets/food/ politics/musical tastes/religious beliefs/ and so on.

If Jesus was among our guests, and who's to say he wasn't, he probably wouldn't have cared about the bed. He'd slept in much worse. What he would more likely care about is our typically American, resource-gobbling life style in an increasingly impoverished, depleted world. He would care that we keep so much of our time and treasure to ourselves. It's something we're aware of, at least, and try to remedy bit by bit.

The Guest Room Bed has been replaced, but the experience was humbling. Joe's comment propelled me into making a reality check. It's also helped me to be more tolerant of hosts' shortcomings when I'm a guest myself.

Hospitality is a good thing, and we will continue to offer it. Come on by!

Thank You God for each guest I have entertained.

Fourteen

Heaven or Hell

September 1996

The time is fulfilled, and the kingdom of heaven has come near; repent, and believe in the good news.
— Mark 1:15

Bill first told me this story. I believe he'd heard it at a funeral.

A man dreamed he had died. He was taken by an angel to a room where food was plentiful, where tables were laden with meat, fruit, vegetables, bread, wine, milk, honey. But the people were weeping and wailing. Spoons were tied to their hands; spoons with handles so long they couldn't bend their arms around to bring them to their mouths, and so the food remained out of reach. They were desperate, and they were starving.

"This is hell," the angel said.

In the other place they visited, the situation was the same—abundant food, long spoons tied to the people's hands. But here the people were happy, smiling, well-fed. Why? Because they were using their long spoons to feed each other.

"And this," said the angel, "is heaven."

Let's imagine that instead of space or walls dividing the rooms there is a short hallway. People can pass easily from one room to the other. Oddly enough, many of the unhappy souls in hell choose to stay where they are. Asked why, they say things like: "This is my spoon. It was issued to me at birth and I've kept it through my own enterprise and good investments. I don't know the people in that other room. Some don't look entirely clean or altogether healthy. What about germs? What might I catch from someone else's spoon? No thank you. I know if I try harder I can get this spoon to my mouth."

But many others do choose to move down the hall, and are welcomed.

The man woke, and this is what he understood from his dream: *There is a time and place where one is free to move between heaven and hell. The time is now, and the place is here on earth.*

Studies find that people who do volunteer work on behalf of others are happier. Not just a little happier—much happier. But won't we be self-serving if we find volunteer work to do just to make ourselves happier? Ah, that's the sneaky part. Why we do it doesn't matter. It's what we do for others that counts, not our motive for doing it. And even if we are skeptical to start with, we don't stay that way.

What exactly shall each of us do? We need to start with a second question: *What unfilled need do I care deeply about?* When we answer the second question, we'll be well on the way to answering the first.

Are we concerned about the mentally ill? Plenty of places want our help. The poor? Again, no lack of opportunity. The marginalization of women? The plight of animals? Of neglected children? The addicted and formerly addicted? The environment?

Next we make that phone call, and follow through. That spoon on our hand will no longer be a burden.

Strengthen me God to come to the aid of others less fortunate than I.

Fifteen

The Sunny Side

January 1997

In the time of King Herod, after Jesus was born in Bethlehem of Judea, wise men from the East came to Jerusalem, asking, "Where is the child who has been born king of the Jews? For we observed his star at its rising, and have come to pay him homage." – Matthew 2:1,2

There's a country gospel song about looking on the sunny side, and a song popular in the 1930's about walking on the sunny side of the street. We're told by another song to brighten the corner where we are. It all seems so facile, so foolish. How can we walk in the sun when so much bad is going on?

But so much bad has always been going on. Dwelling on that gets us nowhere.

Consider the Magi, living in uncertain, troubling times yet deciding to take off for foreign parts to see a baby who might possibly, against all odds, live to be a king one day, and not their own king at that. I can almost hear their friends saying: "So. Hear you're planning a long trip. Going to strange lands among hostile people who don't speak our language. And you'll be following what? A star? To see a Jewish child? Listen, I know some people from down this very street who headed that way ten years ago. Haven't been heard from since. And they were visiting relatives. Look, the way things are these days, if I were you…"

The three Magi didn't listen to the cynics. They followed their intuition, investing their lives in a journey with an end that was by no means certain. They followed their star, and it brought them face to face with God.

Probably they experienced discouragement and doubt along the way, plenty of times, since the trip was said to have taken them about two years. Sometimes clouds and rain must have obscured the star. What's more, their "sunny side" was strictly metaphoric, since bright sunlight would have made a star impossible to see. In the clouds and in the day, they had to travel on faith.

Maybe they talked together on an especially foggy evening after a bright sunlit day. "Can you see it?" "Well no, I haven't seen it lately." "Will we ever see it again?" "Was it ever there to start with?" "All right, so we're not sure. But we need to keep going as if we were sure." So they kept going, and eventually saw God in Jesus, and their Epiphany brought God to the whole world.

We must keep going, too, *as if.* As if everything will be all right. Psychologists say that we can choose our feelings and our world outlook. They say that people who choose to look on the bright side live longer, happier lives. Such people also get more done. Pessimists give themselves leave to opt out.

Optimists do not. Optimists keep on traveling after that uncertain star.

Being Christian means being hopeful. Things look bad but they will get better. We know it in our hearts. God told us so.

Thank You God for Christian hope.

Sixteen

Here to Stay

February 1997

For the Lord is good;
his steadfast love endures forever,
and his faithfulness to all generations. - Psalm 100: 5

Every year Bill and I search for the right Valentine card to give one another. We don't like the flippant ones, nor the overly sentimental ones. One year we came up with the same card. Might as well have saved our money.

This year my card quoted the lyrics of the Gershwin song "Our Love is Here to Stay":

It's very clear our love is here to stay
Not for a year, forever and a day!
In time the Rockies may crumble, Gibraltar may
tumble
They're only made of clay.
But—our love is here to stay!

Bill's card to me showed a heart literally etched in stone. A similar theme, wouldn't you say?

The Gershwin song lyrics are gently ironic. Rocks and mountains last millions of years while humans last a few decades, and then only if we're lucky. Meanwhile we change rapidly, daily. Our lasting attachments are all the more miraculous and amazing because we change so much. Remaining with a spouse, partner, sibling, friend is a difficult thing to do, and when we manage to do it, God smiles.

God is our example of truly steadfast love. God's love is unchanging. God's forgiveness is etched in stone. We know that about God—and that's about all we know. Much as we'd like to box God up, put our words in God's mouth and our thoughts in God's mind, it can't be done. God remains uncontainable and God's ways are inscrutable.

Even God's unfailing love puzzles us sometime. You mean God loves Hitler and the person who wronged us so cruelly as much as God loves us? Oh surely not! But yes, it's true. On second thought, isn't it comforting? What if we mess up badly someday? Do tremendous wrong inadvertently, when we are "not ourselves"? God will love us anyway. God will forgive. God will remain our rock.

Once we recognize that God loves and forgives us, we can set about trying to love and forgive ourselves. We can acknowledge the bad things we've done. We can say "I did it. No one else is to blame. I'm sorry. And I forgive myself." Because one big reason we can't forgive a loved one some wrong they did is that we can't accept our own guilt and complicity in whatever it was. A close friend said hurtful things? Is it just possible you hurt him, too, and hurt him first? It's worth considering. We must acknowledge our mistakes before we can forgive them. Only then can we go on, restored.

So this year our first Valentine should be to ourselves. We can get ourselves a big red heart full of candy, some red roses in a vase, a card with lace and satin, and say, "Self, you were wrong but I love you anyway. You'll do the right thing next time. I know you will."

Then those other Valentines will come easy.

Thank You God for Your promised forgiveness that allows me to leave my wrongdoing behind and go on.

Seventeen

Name This Child

March 1997

A crowd was sitting around him; and they said to him, "Your mother and your brothers and sisters are outside, asking for you." And he replied, "Who are my mother and my brothers?" And looking at those who sat around him, he said, "Here are my mother and my brothers! Whoever does the will of God is my brother and sister and mother." - Mark 3:32-35

We had a baptism at church the other day. How I do love them! The blinking puzzled infant, off her schedule and away from home; the parents and godparents chiming in raggedly as they "Name this child" and then affirm the ancient vows. Or the older person, come later to the faith, self-conscious and nervous. The part that always thrills me is when the Celebrant marks the person's brow with a cross and says: "Elizabeth, you are sealed by the Holy Spirit in Baptism and marked as Christ's own forever."

Wow.

Of course newly-baptized leaves with the same name she came with. But some things have changed. Her family has expanded to include everyone in the church. This is the family Jesus talks about. Also, in some mysterious way, she truly has become Christ's own.

It is comforting to know our names, which are given to us by those who love us most at a time when we are most lovable. But as we grow up, along with our names come family judgments and expectations about who we are and are not, and judgments and expectations can bind uncomfortably. "Play guitar? I don't think so. You'll be a doctor like your dad and like it." "What do you mean, run for office? You'd better stay home with your husband and child the way I did."

Jesus' family had expectations too. They must have wanted him to carry on the carpentry business. To stay home and help his widowed mother. To be normal. Not to go wandering about, making enemies of the powerful, being called crazy by the neighbors. So one day when he was preaching in a room full of non-relatives, his family came and begged him to come home.

Jesus looked around that room and saw all sorts of people: People with money and people with none. The respected and the despised. Slave and free. Foreigners and natives. Men, women, children. People who wouldn't normally meet one another. He introduced a radical idea of what family could mean. Under God's new Rule, family would no longer be defined by who begat whom. A man's worth was not to be decided by his power, money and position. A woman's value was not to be determined by the marriage she made and the number of sons she bore. People with God's peaceable love in common, with serving others in common, with a refusal to judge in common, could be a family that was freeing, not binding.

Not that the regular kind of family was bad. Having mother, father, sibling was still the ideal — but with Jesus, those who might fill those roles were not necessarily blood-related. We mirror that ideal when we welcome the newly-baptized, with smiles and applause, into our hearts and our church family.

Thank You God for my extended, unrelated family.

Eighteen

The Commercial

April 1997

Then Jesus told his disciples, "If any want to become my followers, let them deny themselves and take up their cross and follow me." - Matthew 16:24

Jesus was no salesman, it seems. When he talked to the disciples he promised them self-denial, troubles, a burden, clashes with the world around them. It's a wonder his ideas didn't die with him. Only they didn't. Why? Why would anyone choose pain over pleasure, difficulty over ease? Why would anyone listen to Jesus?

Last night, watching the umpteenth car commercial on television, I imagined one that was quite different. What if we were to see an ad for a car that isn't sporty or big, isn't parked on an impossibly high mountain or negotiating turns in hazardous weather at breakneck speeds. Actually, in this ad it's hard to tell what color the car is, and the design is anything but sleek. The announcer says, "Test drive the Sparrow today!"

A good enough name, we may think, if not exactly inspiring.

"It isn't comfortable and when you drive it you won't always be in control. How fast it goes or where it goes won't necessarily depend on you. It may take you into some distressing neighborhoods. You'll find, once you've started driving a Sparrow, that there's no turning back."

This is the dumbest commercial we've ever seen. We reach for the remote.

"Many in the world may say you can trade your Sparrow across the board for a car that's more powerful, shinier and newer. This new car will take you to the busiest malls, the wealthiest parts of town, the most exciting neighborhoods. But don't make the trade. You'll lose more than you gain if you do!"

We frown, but we set the remote aside and keep watching and listening. The odd little car is backlit now, and doesn't look so bad. The voice continues. "Where the Sparrow takes you is where you need to be. When you drive one, wonderful people will want to ride with you. They will want to be part of your journey and want you to be part of theirs. You may have moments of doubt about where you are going, but if you ask for guidance it's there for you—part of the car's standard equipment. Sometimes your Sparrow will take the bumpy road, but other times it will seem to glide along, humming happily, and you will sing for joy as well! No need looking your Sparrow up in the Blue Book. You will always be certain of the Sparrow's intrinsic worth and of your own."

We don't bother to look for a Sparrow dealership. Of course there is none. No such car exists. The God-guided, self-forgetting, way of life does exist, though, and that was what Jesus was selling.

No wonder so many good people stay in the market for it.

Thank You God for Your driving guidance in my life.

Nineteen

Calm Sea
June 1997

He woke up and rebuked the wind, and said to the sea, "Peace! Be still!" Then the wind ceased, and there was a dead calm. He said to them, "Why are you afraid? Have you still no faith?" - Mark 4:39-40

When TWA Flight 800 crashed off the Atlantic seaboard, among the passengers was a group of teen-agers from one small Midwestern town. A parishioner said to me, "All those young people, all that promise, gone! Where was God?"

I'd like to think God was in the hearts of the doomed passengers, because I believe God was there in the plane with them, and I hope they believed that, too. God was with them, God gathered them home, and God is equally with their grief-stricken relatives.

When the storm raged around the disciples and Jesus in the little fishing boat, Jesus slept. The panicky disciples wakened him and begged him to calm the sea. He was a little cross about that, so after rebuking the wind, Jesus turned and rebuked the disciples. After all, he wasn't to be with them in body much longer. They might as well start now to rely more on each other and their own competence to get out of trouble. He would be with them always, but in spirit. To know that, they would need faith.

Perhaps his very waking calmed the sea for them. Perhaps their fears were quieted because Jesus was alert to share the experience with them—much as children will be quieted when they wake crying from a nightmare to see their parents' faces and hear their reassuring voices. During WWII, the English children who stayed behind in London to face the blitz with their parents fared better emotionally and physically than the ones sent to the country or abroad, out of harm's way. *Mummy and Daddy are here. It's okay.*

Most of the time planes don't crash. Why don't we ask then where God is? Whatever the law might say, acts of God aren't only the lightning strikes and the tornados and the hurricanes and the accidents. Acts of God are also the peaceful sunsets and the birthday parties—and the smoothness of most of our plane trips. God is love and peace and safety. Most of the time God's world is an ordered world, a world to be counted on.

After the crucifixion, when the disciples returned to fishing, they had to rely on their boat-handling skills, and on prayer. I don't know all the things prayer can do, but I do know it empowers the one doing the praying. By recalling to our hearts and minds God's presence and good will for us, prayer frees us from paralyzing worry, calms us, lets us go on with whatever it is we need to do.

Strengthen me God to recall Your quiet presence in difficult times.

Twenty

The Windmill Story

August 1997

Train children in the right way,
and when old, they will not stray. - Proverbs 22:6

On a hot August day in 1907, in Iowa, a five-year-old girl in a long cotton dress and sandals climbed hand over hand up the tall wooden ladder of a windmill. She did it on a dare.

Mother tells it now: "My brother Ralph was a little older than I. One day he was telling me that boys were better than girls. I didn't like what he said, that girls couldn't do what boys did, so I thought, *All right. I'll climb up the windmill the way he sometimes does and show him!*

So I climbed up, and at first I concentrated on getting my feet on the ladder steps. But then, unfortunately, I looked down. Unfortunately, because I got frightened and dizzy. I let go, and fell!

"Luckily I fell into a tank full of water, the trough for the cattle and horses. I did hurt my leg badly, a big bruise where it hit the side of the tank. But I wasn't injured too much because of the water. Ralph was frightened and he yelled and screamed as he ran to the house. He got in trouble with our parents, and he felt awfully bad about teasing me that way. I guess he learned as much of a lesson as I did! On the whole he was a kind, gentle big brother."

Ralph and my mother Blanche were the two oldest in what was to be a family of eight children born to Clyde K. and Hattie Freeman Wylie. Later that same year they relocated to Idaho, where they proved up on a homestead. Grandpa worked hard all day every day to make a living on their dryland farm. Grandma worked hard all day every day to keep the family clean, clothed and fed. Ralph helped Grandpa in the fields, and Mother helped Grandma in the house.

It wasn't all work. In the evenings Grandpa played the violin, Grandma played the piano, and everybody sang.

As years passed and the children scattered we periodically had family reunions, before Grandma and Grandpa died and after. I can almost hear the uncles' voices as they good-naturedly teased one another with a wit that was dry and incisive yet never cruel. As for the aunts and my mother, and my sisters and my many cousins, oh how we could laugh!

Of all the stories of those farm days, the one that fascinated me most was the windmill story. That story presented to me for the first time the possibility of my own non-existence.

"What if you had died when you fell, Mommy?" I asked. "Where would I be?"

"But you see, Caroline," Mother would say with calm and faultless logic. "I didn't die."

She didn't die, and she is with us still, praise God. She has lived to pass on to me, to my sisters, and to many others a precious, strong, hard-working and happy Godly heritage. Those of us lucky enough to know her are forever grateful.

Thank You God for the stories from my family history.

Twenty-one

Abra la Corazon

September 1997

Then the righteous will answer him, "Lord, when was it that we saw you hungry and gave you food, or thirsty and gave you something to drink?"...And the king will answer them, "Truly I tell you, just as you did it to one of the least of these who are members of my family, you did it to me."
— Matthew 25:37,40

A friend in the adult education Spanish class I'm taking is a *dentista misioneria*, a dental assistant and missionary who sometimes goes with a team to a poor village in Guatemala. Mostly what the team does is pull rotting teeth. The villagers can't afford replacement dentures so they have fewer teeth afterwards, but at least their systems aren't being poisoned. She's taking the language class because she hopes to go back to Guatemala, and to be able to say more than: *Abra la boca, por favor. Open your mouth, please.*

She told us that the people there are incredibly poor and also incredibly loving and generous. When the missionary dental team arrived, they were served a chicken dinner. They enjoyed the meal but didn't think too much about it, except to notice that the chickens were scrawny. Later they found out that

72

the villagers don't eat their chickens. The eggs the chickens produce are their main source of income! By serving that one dinner—because they'd heard that North Americans like chicken—they had depleted their resources for the coming year.

The missionary team was astounded, and appalled, by the selfless generosity and community consensus of this. They had come from the U.S. to embody Christian principles, only to be met with an act that made a kind of economic non-sense and a divine love-sense we seldom find outside of the parables.

My friend went on to say that coming home from Guatemala is even harder than being there. After returning to the United States she almost has to hide herself for several days to avoid being repelled by the materialism of her own society. She has trouble not yelling at her children for wanting more and more stuff, and at her friends who take so much for granted. Fortunately, or unfortunately, the feeling wears off soon.

For the rest of us, too. We see news footage of the kind of village she describes, then immediately watch a commercial for a vehicle that costs more money than the people we just watched will ever see, and if the wrongness of that hits us, the feeling soon wears off.

It wears off, but often we're left with a sense of unease, a sense that things are not as they should be.

That sense of unease is good. We need to keep it and work with it. I believe that our discomfort in the face of the great economic disparity among the world's peoples is sent from God, and signals our underlying connection to one another. When one human being hurts we all hurt. In the long run, our unease and what we do about it, individually and collectively, may be what saves us.

Strengthen me God to keep my discomfort at the plight of the world's poor.

Twenty-two

A Tree

October 1997

They put him to death by hanging him on a tree. –
Acts 10:39b

Fall has come, and the myriad tiny leaves on
the weeping birch tree in our front yard are turning
yellow. I love this tree. I've looked at her so long
with affection that I've personalized her. Three of the
natural birch-slashes on her upper trunk show me a
delicate, sad, enduring face.

I identify with her in part as a survivor. Years ago
a tree expert told us she would soon die because of
the deep gouges in her lower back, made by nature

and humans. She didn't die. She kept on doing what she does so well, producing leaves, shade and beauty. She's still here despite her wounds. And despite our wounds, so are you and I.

In Great Falls, we cherish our trees because we live on an arid plain, and most of our trees we've had to plant. We appreciate trees for their rootedness, their stamina, their flexibility, their beauty and bounty. Biblical people, also living in a dry land, appreciated their trees too. One thing Biblical trees symbolize is Eden's garden, a place to be remembered and longed for. Another is the dying that must precede Resurrection. In Acts, Luke reminds us that Jesus was hanged not simply on a cross but on a tree, the ultimate symbol of life, death and rebirth.

Why are trees such a symbol? Because each Fall the leaves go away. Each Spring they return. Too often we think of a leafless tree as somehow impaired, much as we might think of old people as impaired because their looks and abilities differ from the accepted ideal. Yet all conditions and seasons of tree, and all conditions and seasons of humans, are part of God's plan and order in the world. We may look at a wintering deciduous tree and see within it not death but suspended life, altered life, sleeping life. Its Winter form is as real and as natural as is its Summer one. The age-marks of a tree may indicate its time-gained wisdom and tranquility. So may the age marks on an old woman's face.

We wait for the new buds every spring as we wait for the sun to rise in the morning, the day to lengthen at Winter Solstice. We take it on faith that spring will come, and rejoice when it does. Inevitable? No. Nothing in this world is inevitable, including our own continuing existence. I take it on faith that each Spring my tree will begin to show a tinge of yellow-green. When she does I will rejoice, thanking God for her regular renewal—and for mine.

Thank You God for the natural world that teaches me so much.

Twenty-three

The Birds

November 1997

Even the sparrow finds a home,
and the swallow a nest for herself,
where she may lay her young,
at your altars, O Lord of hosts,
my King and my God.
Happy are those who live in your house,
ever singing your praise. – *Psalm 84:3,4*

We have a new bird feeder this year, with a grill around its six feeding stations so that the small birds — the finches, chickadees, sparrows — may eat without being hassled and pushed out by the larger birds.

Birds have always fascinated us because of their beauty, songs, devotion to one another, survival skills and ability to fly. Since they pursue their difficult lives right out in the open, we can watch their daily struggle to eke out an existence despite storms and drought, shrinking habitat, and predator birds and animals. Night and day they labor to meet the demands of their young. Twice a year, many of them launch themselves into space on long flights with no certain outcome. Birds are incredibly tough, and incredibly fragile.

So are we, and we know it, even though sometimes we forget how tough we are, and at other times,
how fragile. If our lives are not quite so public as
are the lives of birds, they are no less difficult. We
too struggle against dangers to make a good life for
ourselves and our families. We are glad to read in
Scripture that God cares for sparrows and for people.
That means hope for us both.

Contemplating birds can be a melancholy pursuit.
So many birds are doomed to be lost, and yet they
go on living and singing and flying and eating and
feeding as wholeheartedly as though nothing at all
threatened them. *Easy for them*, we think. *They don't
know how bad their situation is!* Well no, and neither
do we, really. We have times of discouragement
when hundreds of hazards rise to our minds. We have
other times of confidence when we believe we are
in control and nothing can stop us. Only with God's
help may we come to a middle way.

To a great extent, we are in control of our states of
mind and our emotions. It is my belief that choosing
hope serves us better in the long run. Hopefulness
(*it'll be okay; it'll all work out*) keeps us going,
keeps us productive, lightens our voice and quickens
our step. We may not have the birds' unawareness
as protection, but we have something better. We
have God. With God, we know we live in perilous
times, yet we trust that God will grant us strength
to survive. Thanks to our faith we, like birds, can
launch ourselves out bravely and confidently into
the unknown. Optimism is courageous. In spite of

everything, we do what we must do, and keep right on singing.

Strengthen me God to pursue my life wholeheart-edly, as the birds do.

Twenty-four

The Year the Cat Nearly Died
December 1997

And she gave birth to her firstborn son and wrapped him in bands of cloth, and laid him in a manger, because there was no place for them in the inn . – Luke 2:7

We don't remember many of our Christmas presents as they pile up behind us, let alone the exact year we received them. Perhaps some Christmases are memorable for special presents. But usually we recall certain Christmases because of a crisis met and overcome.

Certainly the first Christmas began with a crisis. A baby born exposed to the weather in filthy streets might well have died. Many did then, as all over the world many do today. True the family found shelter, but it wasn't neat and sweet, as the Nativity scenes show. It was smelly, noisy, chilly and dirty in that stable. Yet that Christmas story had a happy ending, the happiest ending imaginable. Even as it brought so many together for the first Christian family, so it brings our Christian family closer today.

Our own stories do that, too. Here are some of my minor-crisis memories:

The year I was nine and ran a fever (from the excitement, they said, though I question that now). I spent the holiday on the sofa in a daze.

The year the decorated tree fell on Grandfather Roberts, our most formidable and austere grandparent. Finally, even he managed a laugh.

The year my big sister Jean Katharine almost didn't make it home from college because of the weather. I remember how thrilled I was on December 24th during a night snow storm to see the big Greyhound bus stop across the street from our Indiana house and let her off.

The year the temperature reached 20 below in Great Falls, so that Bill and I and visiting sister Edie grabbed the first tree on the lot and came to love it anyway.

The year the plumbing failed on Christmas Eve, when we had a new baby and a house full of company.

The year our daughter Sarah's cat got closed up in the hide-a-bed for a day. Fortunately our daughter Mary sat on that sofa, then hopped right up again. "This couch is moving!" So we investigated, and a ruffled, cross and thirsty cat lived to celebrate the holiday.

I'm sure your family has similar stories. It's wonderful on Christmas to sit around and talk about them. Such stories remind us of our love for one another, and of our shared and precious family history.

Thank You God for our memorable family holidays.

Twenty-five

The Laughter of Friends

January 1998

Faithful friends are a sturdy shelter;
whoever finds one has found a treasure.
Faithful friends are beyond price;
no amount can balance their worth.
Faithful friends are life-saving medicine;
and those who fear the Lord will find them.
- Sirach 6:14,15

The holidays just past are a time not only for family but for friends as well. Who doesn't have beautiful memories of gathered friends, laughing and celebrating together.

Jesus elevated friendship. From the very beginning of his ministry, he surrounded himself with both men and—unusual for those times—women. Often we see Jesus' friends in the context of taking a meal together, in celebration of something or other. His first miracle, changing water into wine at the wedding in Cana, was within the gathered company of friends. You and I have been to a few weddings ourselves and we know that the jokes and laughter are as abundant as the wine. But we don't hear much about laughter in the Gospels. Why not, I wonder?

The Gospels are succinct. Much is omitted. Also, they weren't written until decades after Jesus' death, and maybe the laughter part was forgotten by then. Maybe, although when I look back over the years and the decades and recall dear friends now lost to sight, it's the laughter I remember most. Usually I don't remember the situations that led to the laughter, but I can almost hear the joyous peals of sound we shared. Of course, recalling those best and happiest times somehow makes the separation from those friends all the harder. Maybe it was the same with Jesus' friends. Maybe we don't hear about the shared laughter now because they were too sad later to talk about it. Or maybe the Bible writers thought we would take the Good News too lightly if we heard about the disciples' occasional frivolity. Seeing the deadly seriousness of some so-called religious people today, I can't help but be sorry about that.

Certainly Jesus laughed with his friends. A humorless life is less than full. Little babies laugh spontaneously! If we lose that ability growing up, we have lost an important part of ourselves. Relaxing with others, trusting them enough to be funny around them, is healthy and reflects part of the "sturdy shelter" friends provide. It is part of their worth to us, and ours to them.

The holiday parties are over now. The wine and pop bottles are out in the trash. The leftover food is in the freezer. The furniture is back in place, the carpet vacuumed. The house is quiet again—too quiet. We are apprehensive about the New Year, seeing shadows of coming change and danger. Can we risk gatherings and laughter with so much trouble in the air? Can we risk bringing loved ones together in celebration, only to lose them in the end?

Jesus could do that. We can too, and we must. Let's not wait too long to call our friends together again! They are, after all, beyond price.

Thank You God for friends.

Twenty-six

The Big Fish

February 1998

*But Moses said to God, "Who am I that I should go
to Pharaoh, and bring the Israelites out of Egypt?"
He said, "I will be with you; and this shall be the
sign for you that it is I who sent you: when you have
brought the people out of Egypt, you shall worship
God on this mountain."* – Exodus 3:11,12

For Christmas, I received a Joke-a-Day calendar.
Here's today's:

A child was watching a fisherman. First the man
caught a giant trout but threw it back into the water.
Next he hooked a huge pike and threw it back, too.
Finally the fisherman caught a tiny bass, smiled, and
dropped it into his basket.

"Hey mister," the child asked. "Why did you
throw back the big fish and keep the little one?"

The man said, "Small frying pan."

People in the Bible were constantly protesting
that they couldn't handle the big tasks God gave
them. *I don't speak well, Lord,* they said. *I'm too
old, I'm too young. I'm too burdened by riches, by
poverty, by family obligations. Give me something
less demanding to do, something more in line with*

my limited capacity. In other words, "My pan is too small for the fish I've been handed."

We all limit ourselves when we fail to apply for the better job or sign up for the harder course or volunteer for a seat on the Planning Board or run for the office or spearhead the campaign or speak up on the issue or submit the poem. It's understandable. We dread and avoid failure as much as—perhaps more than—we anticipate and plan for success.

Here's a Bob Mankoff <u>New Yorker</u> cartoon: A line of newly-deceased people is trooping through a door marked: "Abandon All Hope, Ye Who Enter Here!"

Underneath is written: "If you have already abandoned all hope, please disregard this notice."

How sad, to give up before we absolutely have to. We humans are so easily disheartened! Past failures, past rejections and criticisms stick in our minds for years while past successes, acceptances and praise slip through them like water. It's as though we learn only our missteps "by heart" and forget the rest.

God didn't let those protesting people in the Bible stories beg off. They had to do what God knew they could do. God knows the great things of which we are all capable because God made us that way.

I'll bet that fisherman could have handled those first fish just fine—and so can I, and so can you. Today let's listen to what God has to tell us about our own Big One (Dream, Connection, Plan, Project, Task). Maybe this is the day we can begin to reel it in.

Strengthen me God to use my untapped potential.

Twenty-seven

The Face of God

March 1998

So God created humankind in his image,
in the image of God he created them;
male and female he created them. – Genesis 1:27

A benediction concludes: "May you see the face of God in everyone you meet."

Jesus showed us how to do this. It was a big reason why those at the top of the power structure were threatened by him. Their thinking might have gone something like this: *Is Jesus saying that everyone carries the aspect of God? Even the slave, the Greek, the female, the child, the Samaritan, the leper? That I with my wealth and lineage and power and privilege am not so special after all? What if the people start to believe him? Better get rid of him while there's still time!*

I know some wonderful people who easily see God's face in everyone. Unfortunately I'm not one of them. It's so much simpler to dismiss someone or an entire group of people from one's empathy and concern. *Him? Oh, he's always been a jerk Them? You know how they are.* Maybe you do this too. So for those of us who have to work at seeing God in all people, here's a suggestion for a Lenten discipline:

Week One: We start by seeing the face of God in the bathroom mirror every morning. This may be harder on some days than on others.

Week Two: Every day we look for the face of God in at least one benign stranger: the checkout clerk, the child who admires our dog, the young couple down the street working in the yard. To each we say (though probably not out loud, because they might phone the authorities) "In you, I see the face of God."

Week Three: This is the week for friends. Why might friends be more difficult than strangers to see in this way? Because we and they have a history together, a history that may be clouded. In fact, we need to include former friends whom we usually avoid because they have done us an injury, or we them. "I see in you the face of God." Again, we keep it to ourselves, lest we lay on someone a burden.

Week Four: We come to family week. This may be a snap, incredibly tough, or a mixture. God's face is easily seen in the baby and the child, especially when they are behaving well. Some times we can easily see God in the life partner, the sibling, the cousin. At other times, we must do the best we can.

Week Five: Now we seek out acquaintances, perhaps parishioners, who are alone or ill and would appreciate a visitor. A half hour spent at bed or chair side leaves both the visitor and the visited feeling better, as we see God's face in one another.

Week Six: Finally we try to see God in the faces of people who threaten us because they look different, or live or worship in a different way. Some we may see on TV, their faces distorted with hate. Maybe we aren't quite ready to see God in them. No matter. Others on TV, just as alien, show fear and grief. Surely we can identify with that!

It won't be easy, but I'm sure that if we keep to this discipline, we will emerge from it on Easter Sunday with compassion in our hearts.

Thank You God for the assurance that Your image lives in everyone.

Twenty-eight

What's Right With You

April 1998

Then Jesus said to (blind Bartimaeus), "What do you want me to do for you?" The blind man said to him, "My teacher, let me see again." Jesus said to him, "Go; your faith has made you well." Immediately he regained his sight and followed him on the way.
— Mark 10:51,52

In a P. Reilly New Yorker cartoon from some years back, a man in his underwear sits on the examining table as a doctor reads his x-ray. The doctor says, "Basically there's nothing wrong with you that what's right can't cure."

That's what Jesus tried to tell us.

Take Bartimaeus, who cries out to Jesus for help even after he is told by others to shut up. When Jesus answers, he throws off his beggar's cloak and finds his way to our Lord's side—and just like that, sees again!

In my Bible, the section is titled Blind Bartimaeus, and that's how we refer to him. We focus on what was wrong with him. So did the people of his time.

Jesus did not. He asked, *what do you want*, as though there might be some more pressing need than sight on the man's mind, as indeed there might have been.

Yes, Bartimaeus was blind. He also had a lot going for him. We don't know everything that was right with him. We do know he had a strong voice, a good sense of direction, courage in adversity, an independent spirit and certainty of purpose. Not to mention the faith that made him well.

What did he do? Shouted down his critics. Made his way through the crowd to Jesus' side. Threw off the cloak of disability. Asked for his sight. These actions were Bartimaeus' faith. He used what was right with him to heal what was wrong.

Where others viewed their fellow humans as impaired by infirmity, age, gender, beliefs, past mistakes, race, religion or national origin, Jesus saw all around him worthy, talented people who could make themselves whole. The generosity of his vision allowed him to instill vision in others.

During Lent, we may have focused on things about ourselves we want to change. Now that the Easter season is here, we can focus on our good qualities. We can make a list of our strengths and our abilities—some of which, like Bartimaeus's, may have grown out of our woundedness. No one but ourselves will see this list. It's not bragging, but self-encouragement.

Besides, I suspect that God's list of what's right with us is longer than we will ever know.

Strengthen me God to let what is right with me heal what may be wrong.

Twenty-nine

A Butterfly and a Cockroach

May 1998

*But those who wait for the Lord shall renew their
    strength,*
they shall mount up with wings like eagles,
they shall run and not be weary,
they shall walk and not faint.
- Isaiah 40:31

This survey has been reported: When people are
offered a three-week expense-paid vacation for two
anywhere in the world, provided they agree to kill a
butterfly by pulling off its wings, 80% won't do it.

No, of course not. What kind of heartless creep do you think I am? they say. Or words to that effect.

Now here's the follow-up question: For the same vacation, they are asked if they would step on a cockroach. Now 90% say, *Yes, I'd do that. I'd do that without the incentive.*

Anyone who has come upon a platoon of cockroaches scratching and scuttling around the food in their kitchen is likely to agree with that answer. The response to the maiming-a-butterfly question is harder to understand. After all, butterflies only live a few days at best. And a three-week vacation in Hawaii, Europe? What's the problem? I'm not sure I believe this survey. That is, I'm not sure the people who answered the question actually expected the vacation to materialize. But the general idea is sound. We don't deal simply in facts or practicalities, but in the symbolic. We read more than the obvious into the world around us. And that's a good thing.

Probably we identify with butterflies. We associate them with the beautiful flower gardens and sunny summer days of our childhood. We empathize with the fragile and ephemeral beauty they symbolize. When we remember the cocoon, the tiny prison from which the insect freed itself, we may think of the human soul ascending at the time of death, free at last and light as air. Butterflies remind us of the best of what we like to think we are or were or might become.

A cockroach, on the other hand, symbolizes earthbound ugliness and greed. To quote the Encyclopedia Britannica: *Cockroaches damage more than they consume and emit a disagreeable odor.* We don't want to identify with that description, however accurate it might be. In other words, we cherish the butterfly in ourselves and would like to get rid of the cockroach.

Our tendency to read meaning into things is what makes us human. Our language reaches far beyond the basic-needs signs some animals can master. We often think and talk of what is like what. We think and talk of what we cannot see in terms of what we can. Of God, for instance—God who is our eagle, our rock, our mother-hen, our dove, our armor.

So no matter how accurate or inaccurate the butterfly/cockroach study is, I'm encouraged by it. So long as we can see through and beyond the obvious, there is hope for us.

Thank You God for symbols in the material world that point us to the world beyond.

Thirty

Come, Holy Spirit

June 1998

And when Jesus had been baptized, just as he came up from the water, suddenly the heavens were opened to him and he saw the Spirit of God descending like a dove and alighting on him. And a voice from heaven said, "This is my Son, the Beloved, with whom I am well pleased." – Matthew 3:16,17

The bird sitting hunched and unhappy in our back yard tree one chilly May evening was definitely different from those we usually see. She was pale tan with yellow and white streaks, a plume-like crest and orange spots on her cheeks. The sparrows and finches attracted by our wild-bird feeder perched around her, silently staring. They'd never seen anything like this before!

Clearly she was someone's escaped pet. Bill and I stepped out on the deck, coaxing and calling. Soon she fluttered noisily to the top of my head, and I walked her slowly into the dining room.

I phoned a local pet store. "A cockatiel," the owner said. She sighed. "I tell owners to clip their flight feathers so this won't happen. And yes, I'll keep her here while you try to find the owner. You have wild-bird mix? Feed her millet from that."

But we didn't take her to the store right away. Supper was ready, after all. Besides the bird seemed to enjoy our company and the warmth of our house, as well as the millet and water we set out. She also liked our supper table, eyeing the salad, avoiding the chicken (possibly from fellow feeling), edging across the rice bowl and skirting the butter. Mostly she liked walking around on Bill and me. Resting on shoulders. Stepping sideways up and down arms. Once she made her way from the top of my head to my forehead and, large brown eye to tiny black one, we contemplated one another wrong way up.

After supper we put her in a big box for transportation to the pet shop, where she was happy to hop and eat with the other cockatiels. I advertised in the paper and called the Humane Society. When no owner responded, I released her to the pet store and soon got a call that she now has a new home. I still think of her fondly. Sometimes when I look at that branch, I seem to see her sitting there.

The Holy Spirit that empowers us, that brings us hope and inspiration, is often envisioned as a bird—an elusive bird that touches us lightly and then is gone, so that afterwards we can't be sure it was there at all. What if the Holy Spirit were more like that cockatiel? What if it stuck around, directing us in the way to go by flapping in our ears? Spurring us to right action by tugging at our hair with its long yellow toes? Focusing our attention by staring with beady expectant eyes into ours?

It's an intriguing idea, but not likely to happen. So we must continue to be intentional in order to see the Holy Spirit at work in our lives. That's a good thing!

Thank You God for manifestations of the Holy Spirit in my life.

Thirty-one

Heaven Whispering

July 1998

Therefore the Lord God sent (the man) forth from the garden of Eden, to till the ground from which he was taken. He drove out the man; and at the east of the garden of Eden he placed the cherubim, and a sword flaming and turning to guard the way to the tree of life. - Genesis 3:23-24

On a road trip with friends, we drove past the tall white farm house used in "The Horse Whisperer," a film based on the Nicholas Sparks novel of the same name. It's in a breathtakingly beautiful area, in a crook of the Yellowstone River. The area suits the beauty of the story, which tells of a girl and her horse, both damaged almost beyond repair in a road accident, yet in the end restored to health and to one another.

Director and star Robert Redford had the house built especially for the film. Since a lower, more modern, perfectly good ranch house was on the property already, the added house has caused some carping by Montanans. So has the film in general. I've heard people say such things as: *It shows an impossibly romantic notion of our State. People ought to experience Montana in the winter. They ought to try ranching sometime and see what it's like. The picture doesn't even come close to reality.*

The thing is, nobody expected that it would come close to reality. Nobody ever wanted it to. The very charm of the film lies in its depiction of a place that never was or could be. It's set in Narnia, Wonderland, Camelot, The 100 Aker Wood, a dream world of possibility and hope. Where the weather is always perfect. Where desperately damaged children and animals can rise up and run again. Where, in fact, no one is ill. Where good always triumphs over evil, and love lives on and on.

We need our imaginary places. As a child of eleven or so, about to enter that difficult shape-changing time of puberty, I begged God to excuse me from adulthood and instead sign me up for a house in Oz. Needless to say, that didn't happen. But I remember that longing. Sometimes I still feel it.

From an early age we long for a perfect place. Why? What puts the idea into our heads and hearts? Perhaps we yearn for such a place because we have a sure and certain hope, as the prayer book puts it, of paradise. Some say we retain a memory of dwelling with God in Heaven before our souls arrived here on earth.

As a child, I found the concept of heaven boring because I had known very few of its residents. But now I know and love many of them, and so it's heaven I hope for these days.

Meanwhile we locals need to lighten up about the film. In a sense, you and I dwell as far from the land of "The Horse Whisperer" as do the viewers in Tokyo or Sydney.

As far and, praise God, as near.

Thank You God for my hopes and expectations of paradise.

Thirty-two

Close Encounters

August 1998

But God remembered Noah and all the wild animals and all the domestic animals that were with him in the ark. And God made a wind blow over the earth, and the waters subsided. – Genesis 8:1

The weather was perfect the day of our Glacier Park hike, and the flowers were thick and glorious. We marveled at the bristly orange and red paintbrush, the luminous green and cream bear grass, the masses of blue lupine, the white glacier lily. On the trail near Ptarmigan Tunnel, Bill and I and two friends watched as a huge grizzly bear traveled with incredible speed across a mountain face and disappeared over the top. The bear went over the mountain, indeed!

Heading back, I was for the moment leading the group along the trail. To our right, a narrow band of shrubbery topped a sheer cliff. To our left, sunlight gleamed through the leaves of the bushes lining the trail.

Then, suddenly, sunlight gleamed through thick brown fur.

Fur? I blinked and looked again. Sure enough, just behind the leaves, not five feet away, was a large animal with a massive head and small ears. "It's a bear!" I gasped. The other three came to a ragged stop behind me and looked. It was a bear all right.

"A black bear?" "I think so." "I'm not sure. Isn't that a hump on its back?" "Naw." "Well, maybe…."

Now the bear had seen us. Humans and animal gazed upon one another. Bill readied his pepper spray, in case the animal started toward us. When it didn't, we backed up and waited, giving it time and space. It moved ahead cautiously, glancing at us now and then. Soon trees hid the bear, but we knew it wasn't far and we knew it was traveling in the same direction we were. We hesitated to proceed too quickly. Eventually we cautiously moved ahead to where the bushes opened out into a small meadow. There was the bear, a little farther off now, still ambling along searching for food. Someone guessed that it was about two years old and weighed around 250 pounds. A black bear? Probably…

Soon we lost sight of the bear, and finished our hike.

We love to talk about this close encounter. Behind the story lies a hint of danger: man against beast. Were we ever in real danger? You never know with bears.

In the long run, the bears, wolves and other untamed creatures have more to fear from us than we from them, as human populations encroach farther and farther into their habitat. I don't pretend to know the answer to animal management. I do hope we remember, as we try work with the problems, that God not only created the wild animals but cared for them enough to save them from the flood.

Thank You God for all Your creatures that share the earth with me.

Thirty-three

Giving Charity Back

September 1998

Now in Joppa there was a disciple whose name was Tabitha, which in Greek is Dorcas. She was devoted to good works and acts of charity. – Acts 9:36

During the twenty-four years I worked as a Speech/Language Pathologist for the school system, I provided help for students who had difficulty saying certain sounds, or couldn't form sentences easily, or stuttered, or were language-delayed, and so forth. Sometimes they came on their own to my little therapy room. Sometimes I picked them up from their classrooms. When I did that, the other children would see and take note.

I had one second-grade client with a distorted "r" sound whose first name was Charity. Since she seldom remembered to come to therapy on her own, I would often go and fetch her.

Once when I was in a supermarket, a boy of about seven walked up to me, pointed, and said, "I know you. You take Charity."

I said, "That's right," knowing what he meant. But then what he'd said struck me as pretty funny. Take charity? Not me. When I told the story later, I added, "I should have said to him, 'No I don't. I work for everything I have.'"

It was a mildly amusing thing to say. But it wasn't, and isn't, true.

If I don't "take charity" in the classic sense of receiving something I haven't paid for or earned simply out of the goodness of someone's heart, it's because I've been lucky in my life's circumstances from the very beginning. I was born healthy and kept that way, with excellent medical and dental care. I was born into a middle-class American family with a strong work and education ethic. They nurtured me, encouraged me, and sent me to college. I was always able to get good jobs, and I married a man from a similar background who had a good job, too. I took it all for granted. Most of the world, however, does not have a tenth, a hundredth, of what I have, and their unfortunate circumstances are not their doing any more than my fortunate ones are mine.

So yes, I do take charity. I take the charity of a lucky life. What can I do to repay that charity? I can be aware of it, be grateful for it, and do what I can to give charity back.

Strengthen me God to remain humbly thankful for my fortunate circumstances.

Thirty-four

Blessed Oatmeal

November 1998

*Blessed are you, O Lord God, King of the Universe,
for you give us food to sustain our lives and make our
hearts glad; through Jesus Christ our Lord,* **Amen**
– The Book of Common Prayer, p. 835

Oats peas beans and barley grow
Oats peas beans and barley grow
Nor you, nor I, nor anyone know
How oats peas beans and barley grow.
– old English children's song

I've never cared for oatmeal. I've cooked it only a few times, by special request, and never order it from a menu. The texture isn't pleasing to me, nor is the taste. But now oatmeal has a warm place in my heart and memory because of a special breakfast in Boise a few years back.

My Aunt Dorothy was mortally ill with ovarian cancer. She spent her last months in her daughter Kathleen's home, in a part of the living room especially fitted for her with a hospital bed and curtains and a view of the garden. She was also under Hospice care.

One June morning I sat with my tiny aunt (never a large woman, she was much diminished by her disease) watching the Siamese cats and enjoying the roses outside the patio doors as my cousin Kathleen cooked oatmeal, a favorite dish of her mother's. Dorothy was eating next to nothing by then. Every bite Kathleen could coax into her was a victory.

"Do you want some, too?" Kathleen asked me. *Of course not! I never ate oatmeal.* "No thank you."

But fortunately something told me that the breakfast wasn't about my likes and dislikes, or about oatmeal either. It was about communing with a special person who wasn't to be with us long. "I've changed my mind," I soon said. "Yes, please."

That shared oatmeal, with plenty of brown sugar and milk, tasted wonderful. As the three of us dipped our spoons into the steaming bowls, Aunt Dorothy with her usual dry wit spoke of news items from the paper and reminisced about her days back on the farm. She ate a little oatmeal, and then she went back to bed.

It was the last meal she was to eat at any table. Two days later, peacefully, she was gone. Or so it seemed. As Christians, we know that she merely left our sight for a time. We know that we will all meet again. As the rebirth of "oats, peas, beans and barley" is a mystery, so is the mystery of our own death and our own rebirth with God.

By God's grace and holy mystery, what we have seen flourish once will flourish again some day.

Although I still don't eat oatmeal, I'm often grateful for that bowl, that day. All meals taken together in love are blessed, but some are especially meaningful. I expect you've had such meals in your life. At the communion table or away from it, in ways you and I cannot know, sometimes simply eating the fruits of the garden is more than it seems to be.

Thank You God for all meals shared in love.

Thirty-five

Surprised by Christmas

December 1998

*And suddenly there was with the angel a multitude of
the heavenly host, praising God and saying,
"Glory to God in the highest heaven,
and on earth peace among those whom he favors!"*
— *Luke 2:13,14*

"I've always dreaded Christmas," an unmarried
professional woman friend told me recently, "ever
since I was a child. My dad was usually drunk and
late, spending too much on inappropriate presents or
forgetting them altogether. My mother put up a front,
smiling through her tears, but she fooled no one. So
since leaving home I've traveled for the holidays, or
shut my doors and drawn the shades—anything to let
the season pass unnoticed.

"But a few years ago my friend Sally asked me to
her house for Christmas Eve. I didn't feel I could turn
her down, knowing as I did that her husband had died
the previous July from a heart attack. She had a child,
a little girl of six. Jane. I've never felt comfortable
around children, and Jane was certainly no excep-
tion. She was a plain child with a runny nose who
greeted me sullenly only after being prompted by her
mother, then slumped on the sofa kicking her heels as

Sally and I trimmed the tree. The two of us struggled with conversation while listening to Christmas carols on the radio. Sally was clearly fighting for control. When the tree was only half trimmed, she gasped, thrust toward me a silver ball to hang, and ran from the room sobbing.

"When it became clear she wasn't coming back any time soon, I said to the child, 'Well, Jane, it's your tree, so you'd better help me finish up.'

"She made a face, but soon came and hung ornaments on the lower half of the tree while I did the top half. I worked quickly. My plan was to get the job done, then rap on Sally's bedroom door, thank her for her hospitality, and leave.

"But the moment the tree was trimmed and the lights switched on, the child's face changed. Plain Jane became attractive. With one finger she lightly touched as many of the decorations as she could reach, then looked up at me and whispered, 'Don't you love Christmas?'

"I had determined never to lie to a child as I had been lied to, so I said, 'Actually no, not really. I'm a little like your mom that way. Christmas makes me sad.'

"Too late I remembered that the child had recently lost her father. Inwardly I winced, worried that Jane would break down as Sally had. *Nice going*, I told myself.

"But Jane only nodded. 'I know,' she said. 'I mean, don't you love when you're surprised by Christmas?'"

Unexpected tears welled in my eyes and I hugged her around her thin shoulders. "You know something, I guess I do."

My friend went on. "I still don't like the holiday much, but I work less hard at avoiding it. And at least once during the holiday season, I feel something like the transcendent joy you church people talk about."

Thank You God for the joyous surprises of Christmas.

Thirty-six

Nancy's Story

January 1999

*Then you will understand righteousness and justice
and equity, every good path;
for wisdom will come into your heart,
and knowledge will be pleasant to your soul;
prudence will watch over you;
and understanding will guard you.
It will save you from the way of evil,
from those who speak perversely... – Proverbs 2:9-12*

We can't control what happens to us but we can
control our response to what happens. Take Nancy.

Thirteen-year-old Nancy was invited by Alice, a
school and Youth Group friend, to sing in the choir
on Christmas Eve when extra voices were needed.
The practices beforehand were Nancy's first experience with vocal direction, and she thoroughly enjoyed
them. She loved raising her voice to the glory of God.

The actual service went well. But it began late
and lasted long. The young friends found themselves
nodding off, then giggling softly as they woke each
other up.

At the end of the service, an elderly gentleman
sitting behind them in the choir stall leaned forward
to whisper solemnly, "I hope you girls know you are
born singers!"

Nancy had always enjoyed singing pop tunes, but this was the first time anyone had complimented her voice. Determined to take advantage of her talent, she asked her parents for singing lessons. She worked hard, practicing every day. She made the elite high school chorus. In college, she took lead roles in operettas. Returning to her home town for a career in banking, Nancy sang in the city Symphony Choir. At church she led the alto section, was assigned solos, and received many invitations to sing at weddings and funerals. Singing became her greatest pleasure, the focal point of her social life, and her truest ministry and offering to God.

After executing a particularly challenging solo in church one Easter, Nancy was startled to see Alice, who had moved away long ago and was back visiting her family. When Alice congratulated her old friend on her thrilling, inspiring voice, Nancy said, "Really I have you to thank, for inviting me to join the Christmas Eve choir that time. I never would have gone ahead with singing if that man behind us hadn't said what he said."

Alice frowned, obviously puzzled. "You mean when we were goofing off and grouchy old Mr. Edwards called us 'born sinners'?"

What happens to us happens. But if we let God be part of our response, our lives and the lives of those around us will be the fuller and richer for it.

Thank You God for allowing me to hear Your encouragement in the words of those around me.

Thirty-seven

Poor Clare

March 1999

A wise child loves discipline, but a scoffer does not listen to rebuke. - Proverbs 13:1

March 6 is the feast day of St. Collette, who reformed the religious order of Poor Clares in the 15th century, making it the most austere order of nuns in the Roman Catholic church. Poor Clares are strict in contemplation, extreme in poverty, and utterly devoted to prayer, penance and manual work.

On March 6, as on all other weekday mornings, my little terrier-mix Clare will dog my footsteps, begging for an extended outdoor walk until the moment I decide it's too cold and step on the treadmill instead. Then she will snort in disgust and lie curled up on my bed, long nose covered by fluffy tail, eyes reproachful.

Like a Religious, Clare is Poor and Chaste—in her case, poor by definition and chaste by operation. Is she Obedient? That depends on your interpretation. She jumps on guests, demanding to be petted, and sits where she chooses. Sometimes people who meet Clare will gaze off into space and comment casually on dogs they know who have benefited greatly from Obedience School. I don't know why they do this. I'm happy with the way Clare is now. Usually. She's happy with the way she is now, certainly.

When we walk outside, she strains at her leash—biting, growling and leaping to be free—for about the first half mile. (If she were free she could easily be hit by a car or mauled by a larger dog, but she doesn't know that.) She has never enjoyed that first half-mile of our walk because she is fighting her leash so hard. The first part is just as filled with dog-thrilling sights, sounds and smells as the rest, but she'll never know that unless she relaxes and accepts the restraint.

People see religious orders as impossibly strict and confining, much as Clare reacts to her leash. But as Kathleen Norris points out in her book <u>The Cloister Walk</u>, the founders of these orders believed that we humans are capable of boundless dignity and discipline, and that we possess divine gifts from which distractions and bodily indulgences only divert us. With acceptance of our limits, they say, can come great freedom: freedom to reach our deepest selves, to listen to God, to dream up acts of creativity, community and kindness.

Are we, like Clare, missing the beauty of our journey as we strain and bite at the inevitable leashes of occupational, financial, familial and physical obligations? How free are we really, when we find ourselves incapacitated and made stupid by too much food, drink, yelling or yearning? Would more internal acceptance and discipline release us rather than hold us back?

It's something to think about this Lent.

Strengthen me God to accept and appreciate necessary disciplines.

Thirty-eight

A Rainbow on the Page

April 1999

Look at the rainbow, and praise him who made it;
it is exceedingly beautiful in its brightness.
It encircles the sky with its glorious arc;
the hands of the Most High have stretched it out.
- Sirach 43:11,12

"It doesn't take much," we joke, when some small thing has delighted us.

Recently I was visiting our daughter Sarah in Seattle, where it had rained all winter. Suddenly someone in the house cried, "Come look! A rainbow! Hurry!" We dashed out to the porch and stood there together, gazing at the brilliant arc, exclaiming over its clarity and size, until it was gone.

It was gone too soon. They always are. A complaining Noah might have said, "Gee, God, thanks for nothing! Forty days of rain, and only forty seconds of rainbow?" But he never would have said any such thing, and neither do we. Like the poet Wordsworth's, our hearts leap up when we behold a rainbow in the sky. Forty seconds of rainbow is more than sufficient to bring us joy and new hope. We're lucky that way. It doesn't take much for one thing to remind us of another; for something minor to bring a major truth to our minds and hearts.

Are you in a dark space between rainbows? Not long ago I was, until I remembered an inspired gift one parishioner had brought a hospitalized friend: a coloring book and crayons. When I came visiting later that day, I found the patient happily coloring ocean, fish and boat in a seascape, shading and high-lighting in the best advanced-coloring-book style.

As a child, I colored in those books. One of my warmest early memories is of a California afternoon when I was five, sitting with my mother on the flow-ered living room rug as together we colored in the thick black outlines of flowers, animals, princesses, castles. Later, as the mother of young children, I too colored with them, and thoroughly enjoyed it.

So, in my dark space, I tried coloring again. Coloring book therapy, I discovered, is as soothing and heartening for ailments of the mind as it is for those of the body. In a way, it's like a meditation. The brain can be quiet while all the senses except taste are engaged in the task. The round wax stick fits like a memory between the fingers as the hand sweeps over the page with a soft swish, as the familiar fragrance rises. Best of all, life-enhancing color gradually appears where only gray existed before. It's a little like the way color eases into the world at sunrise. It's a little like how color sweeps into the sky after a rain. Not much like, but a little. Enough. It doesn't take much to remind us of God's promise.

Will there be color in heaven? I believe that there will be, or even that heaven somehow is color. Meanwhile, for the rainbow, let us praise God!

Thank You God for life-enhancing rainbows.

Thirty-nine

The Chinese Vases

May 1999

For God so loved the world that he gave his only Son, so that everyone who believes in him may not perish but may have eternal life - John 3:16

Father collected antiquities. My favorites were twin white vases made of fragile egg-shell porcelain, six inches tall, decorated with red and black Chinese warriors. They were always locked up behind the glass breakfront doors.

In third grade we studied China, and I asked to take the vases to school. At first my parents said, "No." But I begged. I would be really really careful! Anyway, the teachers were locking all the exhibits safely away in a display cabinet.

So they let me.

Somehow a boy got into the cabinet, took out the vases to look at, and dropped them. They each broke into a dozen pieces.

I dragged my wretched self home after school that day, carrying the pieces in a box. The accident hadn't exactly been my fault. But I knew how much my father cared for those vases. Now they were ruined because of something I had done.

Mother was sorry, wished it hadn't happened, knew how bad I must feel. I could tell she was no more eager than I was for Father to come home from work.

Together we showed him the pieces in the box. His jaw tightened and his face went white. "I said it was a bad idea!"

I hung my head, wishing I could disappear, or turn the clock back and leave those vases at home.

Mother drew Father aside and they talked in low voices. When they looked at me again, Father said, "These things happen." But I wasn't comforted. Something besides porcelain had been shattered: my own self-image as a good and trustworthy child. That night I cried myself to sleep. When I woke, I dawdled as I got ready for school, dreading the moment when

Mother called me down to breakfast and I must face my parents again.

To my astonishment, they were smiling. "Look in the breakfront, Caroline." I did. Wonder of wonders, the Chinese vases were back on the shelf! I couldn't believe my eyes. Had yesterday's disaster been a bad dream?

No. A closer look showed the dark glue lines, the small hole where a piece was lost. My parents had stayed up for hours, painstakingly gluing those vases back together. They didn't do it to restore their value. That was impossible. They did it so that I could feel good about myself again.

Now I have those vases on my own shelf. Often they remind me of what unconditional love, human style, can look like.

God's love is like that, only better. God's love is large beyond imagining. With God, when we are truly sorry we are utterly restored. With God, we can be the good, trustworthy children we always meant to be.

With God, no glue lines show.

Thank You God for all the love that has been shown me over the years.

Forty

The Bird in the Market

July 1999

Restore to me the joy of your salvation,
and sustain in me a willing spirit. – Psalm 51:12

On a recent Sunday afternoon, I trudged behind my rattling shopping cart through the East County Market, finding what I needed and marking each item off on my list. My heart was anything but light that day. Even something so simple as grocery shopping seemed a chore and a burden.

Bird seed was one of the last items I had to buy. I headed for the pet aisle and located the wild-bird seed on the lowest shelf. But just as I reached for it, a black-headed little song bird hopped out from inside that shelf and whirred away, up and over the detergent aisle, past the cereal aisle toward the dairy wall and the back of the store.

I laughed aloud in delight, watching the bird's progress until it disappeared. When I bent to take a plastic bag to fill my bird feeder, the first one I touched leaked seed. Apparently the bird had pecked through the paper and was eating when I startled it.

How on earth did that bird find that seed? Inside a supermarket, inside a plastic sack? Certainly, migratory birds have marvelous powers of navigation.

Some of them fly hundreds, thousands of miles from the same yard in the South to the same yard in the North and back again. But presumably that's mostly instinct, an urge imprinted in the egg. Supermarkets are another matter altogether.

I'll never know how it found the seed. But here's a lesson I took from what I had seen: if birds can find sustenance under difficult, unforeseen circumstances, how much more can we? Sustenance for our bodies, sustenance for our souls? Even when we walk with heartache, one effortful step at a time. Even when we push or carry a load a heavy load. Even then the unexpected can startle us out of ourselves and our troubles and into joy and hope. We can't predict or control moments like that. We can only be open to them, and be grateful when they happen.

I went back to the store today. The opened bird-seed sack was gone, and the bird was nowhere in sight. I hope it flew out a front door or a delivery door and is free now. Who knows, one of the birds at my feeder might be that very one. I know it likes the brand of food I buy. The idea makes me smile.

Thank You God for unexpected messangers of hope.

Forty-one

The Raspberry Patch

September 1999

O how abundant is your goodness
that you have laid up for those who fear you,
and accomplished for those who take refuge in you,
in the sight of everyone! - Psalm 31:19

A few months ago, at the height of summer, I could see the crimson gleam of our raspberries from the kitchen window. Many mornings I would take a colander and my brimmed hat and go out to the garden. Under the bright hot sun, I would hold the container under the laden branches. With three fingers I would gently tug the softly corrugated red-purple berries so that they plopped almost by themselves into a pillowy heap. Some of the berries fell to the ground and some were bird-nipped and ragged, but I didn't mind. There were plenty of extra berries for both earth and sky creatures. Plenty for the two neighbor boys who came respectfully to the door.

"May we pick today?"

"Yes indeed! The two of us can't eat them all."

But now August is almost over. This morning I had to search hard for edible berries, and my fingers were chilled by the metal colander and the cold fruit.

I shivered. Where was the sun, anyway? Wasn't it late this morning?

As I turned to the East, there it was. Filtered through the neighbor's still-green tree, the sun made shimmering yellowed lace of our corn tassels and glittered on the few precious raspberries that remained. Flooded by a sudden sense of well being, I stood very still, keeping the moment as long as possible.

Soon the raspberries will be only a memory, the lush bushes bare stalks, and snow will cover the garden. But the shape and place of the garden will remain, because even lying dormant, a garden is a garden. Through the long cold winter, that marked-off corner of our yard will be both a memory and a promise. It will be a reminder that one day Spring will come, and Summer will follow. We know that if we know anything.

Sometimes in our lives the abundance of God's goodness seems to dwindle and chill like that berry crop. But God's bounty, unlike that of the garden, is not tied to the seasons. We need only wait and watch, and hold on to our faith. Because sooner or later, often at unexpected times and in unexpected places, God's grace and goodness will burst forth and fill our hearts to overflowing.

Strengthen me God to keep summer memories warm in my heart as winter comes.

Forty-two

The Song of Harvest Home

November 1999

Come, ye thankful people, come,
raise the song of harvest home:
all is safely gathered in,
ere the winter storms begin;
God, our Maker, doth provide
for our wants to be supplied;
come to God's own temple, come,
raise the song of harvest home.
— Hymnal #290, Words by Henry Alford

Bill and I will have more people than usual gathered around our Thanksgiving table this year. So many in fact that we'll need to hold our elbows close to our sides while we eat. That's all right. It's more than all right; it's a real blessing.

It's not been a wonderful year for our family. For us, and perhaps for you, the year has brought sorrow as well as joy, bad news as well as good. When the bad seems to outweigh the good, coming together in order to be God's thankful people is more difficult to do. The work involved, the socializing required, seem to loom before us. But simply making the effort helps bring us out of depression. The very difficulty of gathering makes gathering vital.

Take the Pilgrim mothers and fathers, that first Thanksgiving Day. Yes, they'd had a fine harvest, and they'd made new friends in the Native Americans who had helped them. But the winter preceding the feast had been cruel beyond our imagining. Of the 100 or so original settlers, only about half survived. Everyone at that First Thanksgiving table was grieving many others — their lost children and parents, husbands and wives, sisters, brothers, dearest of friends. Many of the survivors were still sick and weak. They might justifiably have been sunk low in despair, might have huddled separately in their small dark houses. They might have spent their time longing to return to civilization in England and dreading the snows soon to come. After all, they had no reason to expect that the coming winter would be any better than the last one had been.

But the Pilgrims didn't sit around in self-pity and bitterness. Those who were left alive and well enough came together to eat, sing, laugh and pray. Together they thanked God for the blessings they still enjoyed, the blessings they hoped would come. They prayed to be worthy and they prayed for strength.

We can do that. I don't know what sort of year you have had. Chances are you too have experienced withering storms as well as bountiful harvests. But right now, today, we are all right, you and I. We are doing okay. Let's thank God for that. This Thanksgiving, let's gather with our friends and family, grateful that together we have weathered much. Winter storms will soon begin. But with thankful hearts, and by the grace of God, we will see them through once more.

Thank You God for Thanksgiving company past and present.

Forty-three

Good Lord, Deliver Us

December 1999

From ghoulies and ghosties and long-legged
beasties
and things that go bump in the night,
Good Lord deliver us. – *Old Scottish prayer*

We were happily walking along, my little dog Clare and I, enjoying the unseasonably warm morning. I was daydreaming about something or other, and only vaguely aware of a couple standing in their doorway, talking.

Suddenly their huge bulldog plummeted from the front porch across the small lawn right at Clare!

He must have weighted sixty or seventy pounds. She weighs twelve. She strained to the end of her leash so I couldn't reach her to grab her up. The couple in the driveway called a name, but that didn't stop the animal. In an instant it was on Clare, engulfing her. Picturing those great teeth puncturing her fragile neck, chest, head, I screamed. Finally the couple was there, dragging their dog back. It took both of them. Sobbing at the narrow escape, stumbling in my distress, I snatched up Clare, held her close and walked as fast as I could toward home.

I think maybe the bulldog was new to the couple, or the couple new to the neighborhood, and they didn't realize what could happen. I don't know. I do know I'll carry Clare when we go by there again. If we ever again go walking at all.

What struck me once again was how quickly our seemingly quiet, ordered and controlled lives can change. We think we're managing fairly well, budgeting our time and money, balancing our days. Then, without warning, one bright morning a dog rushes out. A heart falters. A car looms from nowhere. A pain stabs. A call comes from the police. Chaos!

We try our best to keep ourselves and our families safe and healthy, to stave off disaster, but in this uncertain world our best can only go so far. So much is out of our hands.

What can we do? We can keep a close hold on our faith and hope. We can remember that from chaos God creates order over and over again. We can recall during this holy season how good things as well as bad arrive suddenly. Angels appear to Mary, to the Shepherds. A Star appears in the East.

Then, when trouble comes, we can hug God's promise to ourselves, sob and stumble if we must, gain our feet again, and keep walking on toward Home.

Thank You God for deliverance from dangers.

Forty-four

Angel Name

January 2000

*After eight days had passed, it was time to circumcise
the child; and he was called Jesus, the name given
by the angel before he was conceived in the womb.*
- Luke 2:21

January 1st, eight days after Christmas Day, is
the Feast of the Holy Name. It is the day that Mary
named her baby, as the angel had told her.

The new year has been portrayed as a baby as
far back as the ancient Romans and Egyptians. But
Christianity reminds us that what is new is not the
year. *We* are what is new. Because Jesus was born,
we can be re-born, if only we want to be. If only
we re-think ourselves and turn from our old ways,
resolving to lead a new life, we can be as fresh and
free as a baby.

But that's hard to do when we wake each morning
the same old self with the same old name, carrying the
same old load of troubles and regrets on our backs.

Let's pretend the Millennium pessimists were in
fact right. Let's pretend our names were erased from
all the computers on January 1st. Imagine that it's
1900, and almost none of us is born yet, let alone
named. The situation isn't all that bad, now is it?

What would you do differently if your name were erased and you were beginning right now? For starters, what brand new name would you want your angel to give you?

Go ahead, pick one. It could be a name you find pleasant to the ear: Algernon. Marianna. It might be the name of a beloved friend or relative: Reine. Brian. Or the name of a person you've never met but have admired: Abraham. Oprah. It could be descriptive like a Native American name: Daughter of the Buildings that Scrape the Sky. Son of the Fish-filled River. It could be from a book: Rhett. Scarlett.

Now take that name and, for a few hours at least, make it your own. Live inside it. I'll pick Abigail— who happens to be wiser and stronger and more sure of herself than Caroline ever was. That means I can throw away stuff that belonged to the old Caroline. I can get rid of all the sad or embarrassing memories, all the small and large mistakes, all the hurts inflicted on or by Caroline over the years. Wow. That feels wonderful. And why not, when God has made all things new! You try it too. Toss all that unnecessary stuff out. Let it go. Delete it. It belongs to someone else entirely.

There now. Isn't that better?

Happy New Year, whoever you are!

Thank You God for making all things new.

Forty-five

Waxwing Memories

February 2000

We thank you for setting us at tasks which demand our best efforts, and for leading us to accomplishments which satisfy and delight us. – The Book of Common Prayer, p. 836

Our back yard is fenced so that our little dog Clare can run freely. One spring a pair of waxwings discovered our neighbor's tree, and nested there. These birds were fiercely protective of their young. They saw Clare as a threat, even though she couldn't possibly have gotten through the fence, let alone climbed a tree. Every time she went out, they noisily circled and dove at her, endangering her head and eyes with their sharp beaks.

Clare reacted with bewilderment and fear. She didn't understand where the attacks were coming from or why they were happening. Soon she became afraid to venture off our deck alone. I had to coax her down as I shouted and waved the birds away. Even after the waxwings left for the winter, even after their nesting tree became diseased and was cut down, Clare hesitated and cowered. It was a year or two before she forgot about the waxwings and happily ran down the deck stairs to roam her backyard queendom once again. Even without the noisy evidence, she stayed frightened.

Of course, we logical humans never over-generalize or exaggerate our difficulties the way our little dog did.

Or do we.

A little girl forgets her piece during a piano recital and has to start over. Another child sniggers. Her response: *I can't play well enough, so why try?* And she abandons her lessons. A young woman longs to help save the whales, tries fund-raising and is mocked by someone. *Okay, no more causes for me.* A student teacher, inspired by his math professor to teach math himself, has trouble disciplining his first class. *I'm no good at teaching after all.*

Too often we take to heart every offhand criticism, every minor attack. Too often we never try again to do something we once loved.

But God give us our talents and passions, and means for us to use them. When we catch ourselves thinking, *I'd love to do that but I know I can't*, let's recall our lives and see if there isn't a hurtful, waxwing memory back there somewhere. Chances are good that there is. Chances are also good that not only are those birds long gone, but so is the tree they nested in!

Chances are good that now's the time to try again.

Strengthen me God to use my abilities despite painful memories of failure.

Forty-six

In a Butte Hotel

March 2000

Do not judge, so that you may not be judged. For with the judgment you make you will be judged, and the measure you give will be the measure you get.
- Matthew 7:1,2

Lent is here again. It's time to give up something we wish we didn't do, like smoking, or drinking or eating too much. Or to take on something we wish we did do, like exercising or dieting. Occasionally such disciplines seem irrelevant and trivial. Why would God care if we want to damage our health? It's our loving others that God cares about, right?

For one thing, God wants each of us to be the best, most complete person we can be in order to do God's work. But it isn't only that. God wants us to be the best we can be so that we can like ourselves. Otherwise our perception of others tends to be obscured and distorted by our negative perceptions of who and what we are. It's called "projection," this displacement of our own feelings onto someone else, and it causes much of the trouble in this world.

Years ago Bill and I were in Butte, staying at the Finlen Hotel. He was attending a legal conference and I was seeing the sights. In the evening we were to meet for dinner. So around 5 o'clock I dressed myself up in my new teal dress and went down to the lobby to wait.

I smoked in those days, and that is what I did, lighting a couple of cigarettes in a row to pass the time.

Soon I noticed an older woman sitting across the lobby staring at me. *She wants me to put out the cigarette*, I thought. *Well, too bad! If she doesn't like it she can go sit somewhere else.* So I smoked and she stared, and the more she stared and I smoked the worse she looked. Disagreeable. Sour-faced. A spoilsport. Eventually she stood up and began to walk toward me. Was she actually going to come right up and talk to me? She was! I defiantly flicked some ash from my cigarette into the ash tray, lifted my chin, and waited.

As the woman approached me, she began to smile. Automatically, I smiled back. She said: "I've been admiring your dress. Did you buy it here?"

So I relaxed, put out my cigarette, thanked her, and we talked, and she was a lovely person, really.

I hadn't been able to see her clearly because my vision was so clouded by my negative feelings about my own bad habit. My own smoke got in my eyes. I had given to her the mean thoughts that by rights belonged to me.

Not too long afterwards I quit smoking, and my vision cleared—at least about that.

It happens a lot, I think, that we try to paste our guilt on other people. Maybe we can't give up everything we dislike ourselves for doing, or take on everything we believe we should do. But when we change just one thing important to our self-image, we give other people that much more chance with us.

Strengthen me God to see other people clearly.

Forty-seven

My Mother's Cat

August 2000

God saw everything that he had made, and indeed, it was very good. - Genesis 1:31a

When Mother moved to my house from Cambridge Court Assisted Living some weeks ago, her little calico cat Kristy came with her.

I didn't much want Kristy here. Her claws are sharp, and she applies them to legs and furniture. Her long white, black and brown fur sheds. Her purr is so quiet you can barely hear it. She came to a household that feeds birds, and that keeps a dog. Worst of all, our daughter Sarah, who visits sometimes, is allergic to cats.

A few days after she arrived, Kristy ran outside and disappeared.

Oh well, I thought. *One less worry.*

Then I thought back to the years when Father worked in Washington D.C. for the State Department and we lived in Alexandria, Virginia. A wild area lay beyond our back yard, a wonderful place with lush trees, thick undergrowth and a stream. Our cats loved it back there, as did we children.

I was nine years old when this incident happened.

One day our cat Double didn't come home. Days passed, and still no cat. I didn't think Double would be missed very much. She was hard to distinguish from her sisters Mickey and Ditto. She had stripy, cat-color fur, a standoffish disposition and a strident mew. When I saw how anxiously Mother looked for that cat, I was surprised. I wondered at it.

Ten days after the cat's disappearance, I glanced up from the breakfast table and there was Double, standing on the sill outside the window, wringing wet and yowling.

"Look, Mommy!"

Mother looked. Mother laughed with relief, threw open the window and lifted in that dripping, squirming animal. Wrapping it in a towel, she alternately rubbed and hugged it. "Double must have been caught on the other side of the stream! She finally had to swim over! Imagine!"

Since Mother was rarely demonstrative, I was mightily impressed by that warm welcome. After mulling it over I decided that if I, who knew myself to be a self-centered, plain and sometimes troublesome child, were to get lost and then return, Mother would be that happy to see me again! Maybe even happier. I felt glad about that.

Surely God means us to tend and care for every living being that comes under our protection, even when that being isn't one we would have selected given a choice. If this were not so, the less attractive and desirable of us would be abandoned much more often than we in fact are.

So when Mother's cat Kristy came back, as she did in within twenty-four hours—before Mother had even missed her—I picked her up and held her softly vibrating, warm furry body against my ear. "Well now. There you are! Welcome home."

Luckily Kristy doesn't bother the birds, and the dog tolerates her. She's out much of the time, so she sharpens her claws and sheds somewhere else. As for what happens when Sarah visits, I guess we'll improvise.

Thank You God for every living thing You have placed within the circle of my care and concern.

Forty-eight

Homesteading 1907

September 2000

For our daily food and drink, our homes and families, and our friends,
We thank you, Lord. - *The Book of Common Prayer p. 837*

My mother, Blanche Wylie Roberts, is 98 years old today, August 23.

When she was five, the family moved from Iowa to Idaho, to prove up on a homestead. A few years ago I talked with her about her life. "Tell me about your homestead." This is some of what she said:

"We went West on the train. Some of our favorite horses and a cow and our furniture went along in a freight car.

"We had a very small shack way out on the prairie. They didn't call it a desert, but it was desert-like. Sagebrush. We children would go out and look at the sagebrush. We were so excited when we found cactus flowers! Everything else was dull, sage-colored. But the flowers were beautiful, waxy, various colors. Pink and yellow.

"It was a little community. There were four houses, built where people's land intersected so they would be together. They would help each other with anything that needed to be done, including building their houses.

"Those first houses weren't much. There were no basements. The houses were up on supports. Most of them weren't even painted, just bare wood. We had an upstairs of a sort, although it was more like an attic. The children slept up there. We didn't have regular stairs, we had halfway between a stair and a ladder. It had not very big rungs and a little bit of railing. We had mattresses on the floor and nice, regular bedding – sheets and blankets that we had brought. Mother and Father had a bed downstairs.

"Potatoes were a good crop there. We lived on them. We had potatoes every day, sometimes for breakfast. Of course, before you could plant anything, you had to take off the sagebrush. That was a terrible job! Roots, you know. The men and boys had to go out and grub—that is, take off the sagebrush, pull up the roots. So it took a long time to get much land to work with. That's why Father taught school, because he just didn't have enough land to feed all his big family.

"We couldn't go to church much at our first homestead. We used to get together for worship at each other's houses. We'd take turns. They used to come to our house a lot because we had a piano. We'd get together and read a little bit from the Bible, and then sing hymns. There was a traveling preacher who used to come through once in a while, to baptize the children.

"We didn't have much but we were a wonderful family. All eight of us children and my mother and father. A wonderful life, really, hard as it was."

A happy childhood is a great boon and blessing that helps us through whatever is to follow. Those of us who were happy as children can show our gratitude by helping those children who come under our influence toward their own happiness.

Strengthen me God to make glad the childhood of young people near me.

Forty-nine

To Hear the People Pray
December 2000

Jesus said, "Let the little children come to me, and do not stop them; for it is to such as these that the kingdom of heaven belongs." - Matthew 19:14

Pattiann Bennett, a second-year Ministry Formation student in the Montana Diocese, gave me permission to share this story with you. I have changed the name of the child.

"Our church in Eureka is not a young church. We don't have a Sunday School because there are no families attending with children. A few weeks ago, I was at the church on a Friday, cleaning up outside. A little boy around 8 years old named Andy came walking by and wanted to know if the church was open. I said it was, and would he like to come in and see it? He did come in and looked all around. Then he asked if there was a Sunday School. I said there would be, if he came. He said he wanted to come and hear the people pray. He said he wanted to sit in the front row so he could see me and see what was going on.

"I saw his mother outside that day and asked her, and was not met with great happiness about it because they sleep in. Well, that Sunday I hoped

Andy would come and I waited for him, but he must have slept in.

"Two weeks later, as the priest and I were standing inside the door waiting to process in, we watched the big red door being slowly opened by a little hand folded over the edge of it. A little blond head of hair peeked in, and here came my little friend—barefooted and in his pajamas. It was 32 degrees outside. He had wakened on time, on his own—no one at home even knew he was gone—and ran to church barefooted and in his jammies to hear the people pray.

"So Andy sat on the steps leading to the sanctuary, quietly taking it all in. The yellow morning sunlight was streaming through the windows onto the red carpet. From where I was at the altar, I could only see his little bare squirming feet on the steps in the light of the sun. They were Jesus' feet for a moment.

"With permission he ran up to me beside the altar and nestled in there. For the rest of the service, he was the vision of reverence with head bowed and hands folded, his natural and holy priestliness blessing us all by reminding us of exactly where we are, who we are, why we were there, and why we are here. We were all enriched by his small presence."

Thank You God for the children of the church.

Fifty

Call Your Mother

January 2001

O Lord, in the morning you hear my voice;
in the morning I plead my case to you, and watch.
- Psalm 5:3

I woke and prayed, *Please God, let me hear from Sarah today.* I'd been praying the same prayer for weeks and weeks, with no response.

Months earlier, on a bitter January day, Bill and I had put our older daughter on the plane in Calgary, Alberta, bound first for England and then for a meditation pilgrimage in India. She looked so small, so vulnerable, and even younger than her 28 years. *I may never see her again,* raced through my mind—not only then but many times after that, as I tried to think of other things.

A while later, she sent a card from a place called Bodhgaya to say that the pilgrimage was over and that she was striking out on her own. She was headed for the north of India. "I'll stay in touch, Mom."

But she hadn't stayed in touch, and whenever I thought about the things that can happen to a young woman alone I shuddered and my stomach ached.

One day, cleaning a desk drawer, I found a torn-off piece of brown wrapping paper with the name of the meditation center in London where Sarah was originally bound. Should I call? What if I did call, only to hear bad news? I paced the kitchen a few times, then prayed for strength and picked up the phone. Not used to overseas calling, I made some false starts before reaching someone at the other end. "Sarah Conklin?" the English voice said. "No, I don't know her. We see so many Americans." *(Too many,* his tone implied.) But I couldn't let him go.

"She was with Christopher's group."

"Yes? He's somewhere in Asia so far as we know. But I'll try to pass the word along. Ta." He hung up.

My shoulders slumped as I hung up the phone. That was that. At least I had done something.

Three weeks later, the phone rang. I picked it up.

"Mom?"

That beloved voice! Faint and far away, yes, but unmistakable. The wave of relief that washed over me was so overpowering I had to sit down.

"Sarah, how are you?"

"I'm fine. I'm in Dharmasala. I'm sorry not to call before, but calling is expensive and phones are hard to find."

"It's wonderful you called now! I've been so worried."

"You know, Mom," she said, "a funny thing happened. I was sitting in a teahouse drinking *chai* and eating chocolate cake. It's what my friends and I usually do in the afternoon. A woman came out of the shadows and bent down to me. She whispered in my ear, 'Call your mother.' Then she walked away. We'd never seen her before or since! Anyway, I thought I'd better phone."

"I'm so glad you did!"

Who was that woman? Had my call to England brought her there? I don't suppose we'll ever know. But when I prayed that day after Sarah's call, God was the One I thanked. Because when we make even the smallest of moves toward what we need, God responds—often through other people, often in ways beyond our understanding.

Thank You God for Your unrecognized angels.

Fifty-one

The Sleeping Giant

February 2001

For the mountains may depart
and the hills be removed,
but my steadfast love shall not depart from you,
and my covenant of peace shall not be removed,
says the Lord, who has compassion on you.
- Isaiah 54:10

Every few weeks for several years now, I've been driving the 90 miles back and forth from Helena as I co-lead the Diocesan Ministry Formation Program with the Rev. Dr. Brady Vardemann. On my way home not long ago, I saw the Sleeping Giant. (The Sleeping Giant, of course, is that portly, mountain-formed supine fellow with the comically bulbous features best seen from the Helena side of the Big Belts.)

So I saw him and I smiled. "Well, hi there!" I said. "Have you been away?"

Not surprisingly, he didn't answer. He was sleeping.

The Giant was familiar enough, because I'd looked at it dozens if not hundreds of times in the forty-plus years I've lived in Montana. But last week I realized it had been a year, maybe more, since I'd brought the Sleeping Giant to consciousness. I'd driven right on by him with other things on my mind.

The mountain range itself is always on my mind as I approach the Wolf Creek Canyon. Winding, steep driving isn't something I enjoy. In good weather, I slow down for the curves, though plenty of people don't. In bad weather, I grit my teeth and really slow down. I can't ignore the mountains any more than I can the other difficulties, obstacles and worries of my life. So why hadn't I seen the Sleeping Giant? Huge and obvious as it is?

Here's the reason: While mountains are impossible to ignore while one is driving through them, going that extra mental step and making out the human face and form in the mountains takes intention. I hadn't seen it because I hadn't tried to see it.

The moment I recalled it to mind, there it was. Reassuring. Unchanging.. Solid.

It occurred to me that, like the Sleeping Giant, God is always with us but not always brought to our minds. There the resemblance ends. The Sleeping Giant is merely a rock formation while God is God, more fully living than we can possibly imagine, and constantly aware of us. God's steadfast love never leaves us. It's just that sometimes we go for long stretches of time being thoughtlessly unaware of God's presence and of God's sustaining love.

All we need do to connect again is to open our inner eyes, look, and smile. "There you are, God! I guess I've been away."

Thank You God for Your constant, sustaining presence in my life.

Fifty-two

Surviving

May 2001

"Arise, my love, my fair one, and come away;
for now the winter is past, the rain is over and gone.
The flowers appear on the earth; the time of singing
*   has come,*
and the voice of the turtle dove is heard in our land."
- Song of Solomon 2:10b-12

With spring come reminders of the earth's beauty and bounty.

Herbert had recently lost the woman who was the center of his life for thirty years. One night, after cooking and half-eating a lonely supper, he could barely summon the strength to wash the dishes. He thought, *When this is done I'll watch whatever's on TV. In three hours I can go to bed and try to sleep.* But as he worked to clean his one plate, fork, serving spoon and pan, a large bubble rose from the sudsy dishwater and floated across the room. The sight caught at his heart. He stopped washing and watched, marveling at the tiny rainbow within the transparency until the bubble burst. He remembered something Ida used to say when he was impatient to move on to the next thing. *What's your hurry? Smell the roses, sweetie. They won't last long.* He took heart from the memory, and began to enjoy the other bubbles, the warm slick water, the smoothness of the plate. *I'll take a walk now,* he decided. *Then I'll call Fred and see what's up with him.*

Angela's poor health and financial setbacks forced her to move from her beautiful house into two small rooms. One day she came to the realization that she would never be able to go back; that these two rooms—or some place even more restrictive—would be her home until she died. Her heart sank, and she could barely breathe. But then her eyes fell on the flowers a friend had brought that morning, bright yellow daffodils catching the setting sun through the window. For a long moment she was held by their familiar clear lines, their brilliant color. Gradually but surely, she began to feel better. *It's fine here, she thought. Really. I'm safe and I'm cared for, and it's fine.*

What Herbert and Angela had done was pay attention to the moment. When we pay attention we know this truth: *Although Here and Now are all we have, Here and Now are enough.*

"I used to think of grief as a deep hole that I had fallen into and might never get out of," Patricia, who had lost her four-year-old son to leukemia, said. "Now I think of it as a wave that washes over me. While I'm under and surrounded by it, I despair. But if I simply sit still, hang on, and pay attention to the moment, the wave will pass. Oh, it will come again and again, perhaps for the rest of my life. But I know I will have lovely moments, too, many of them. I'll be okay."

Strengthen me God to hold fast during the despairing times of my life.

Fifty-three

Fond of Me

June 2001

Jesus loves me! This I know,
For the Bible tells me so.
Little ones to Him belong
We are weak, but He is strong.
– Words by Anna B. Warner, 1860

A young priest and an old man were walking together along a country road in Ireland when a violent storm came up. Quickly they took cover in a deserted barn as the wind and rain raged around them, rattling the barn's old timbers. When they had found a dry spot, the old man looked up at the dark sky showing through the holes in the barn ceiling and said, "Well, God, here we are. We've found shelter and we thank you for that. We're ready for what you have planned for us now." And he promptly went to sleep on a pile of hay.

But the young priest stayed nervously awake, saying his rosary over and over and wincing at every howl and buffet of the wind. Presently the storm abated, and the old man woke. Assessing the situation he smiled and looked up again. "Well, God, thanks for seeing us safely through another storm."

They walked on. Soon the priest ventured a comment. "You seem to be unusually close to God."

The old man nodded. "Yes," he said. "God is very fond of me."

What a wonderful thought! While some forms of love can be demanding or smothering, fondness is nothing like that. My dictionary defines "fond" as "hopeful and credulous to an absurd degree." It brings to mind the love of a grandparent, that steady, unwavering warmth that comes from the perspective of years and space and cannot be altered no matter what we do.

There are times when it seems that God's unconditional love for us couldn't possibly remain unbroken—times when we've disappointed ourselves and other people too, when we've slipped so badly we can only say, "How could God possibly care for me now?" But God does, because God knows what we're capable of doing and being. God knows we can be as good and as fruitful as we aspire to be in our most optimistic moments. God knows we try.

It's graduation month. I know several graduates, so I have cards to write. Do I need to tell them that they've reached a critical point in their lives, that many fearful storms will rage around them? No, probably not. They know that already, as best they can know it at their age. Better to say something like this: *Do the best you can. Believe in yourself; follow your dream. Remember, God is very fond of you!*

Thank You God for Your fond, unchanging love.

Fifty-four

Television Saint

August 2001

You show me the path of life.
In your presence there is fullness of joy;
in your right hand are pleasures forevermore.
– Psalm 16:11

    August 11 is the day of a favorite saint of mine, Clare of Assissi, who founded the Order of Poor Clares soon after she left home to follow Saint Francis in 1212. August 31 is the 71st anniversary of the first home reception of television, which happened in 1930. Improbable though it may seem, there is a connection. In fact, on top of my large-screen TV stands a four-inch white plastic image of Saint Clare, gazing out into the room.

Clare was a rich and beautiful young woman. One day she heard Francis of Assisi preach a sermon that spoke to her kind and gentle heart; a sermon about the need for detachment from things and money. From then on, she changed her manner of life. She gave him her money to use for charity, and begged to belong to his order. Even though she was female and therefore ineligible to join, he placed her first in a convent and then in a small dwelling beside a church. From there, for forty years, she and the women who eventually joined her devoted themselves to doing works of mercy for the poor and the neglected. The Order of Poor Clares, both the Roman Catholic and the Episcopalian, carry on her faith and work.

Toward the end of her life, when Clare was too ill to attend Mass, an image of the church service appeared on the wall of her room. She said she could see and hear the singing in the church just as though she were present! That is why, in 1958, Pope Pius XII proclaimed her the Patron Saint of Television.

It's amusing to have a tiny plastic saint sitting atop our big-screen TV. It is also a reminder that all our time is God's time, not just the time spent praying or attending church or accomplishing good works. Our leisure time, including that spent watching TV, is God's too. Sometimes she seems to be saying: *Why are you watching this ridiculous farce instead of being with your family and friends? How can you witness this human disaster taking place halfway around the world and not plan to do something about it?* She's right, and it never hurts to be reminded of what we know perfectly well but find easy to forget: that only the joys and pleasures founded in God can give us lasting satisfaction.

Strengthen me God to monitor my television watching through the day.

Fifty-five

A Promise

October 2001

*But know this: if the owner of the house had known
at what hour the thief was coming, he would not have
let his house be broken into. You also must be ready,
for the Son of Man is coming at an unexpected hour.*
– *Luke 12:39,40*

On TV they're showing photographs of people
missing since disaster struck the World Trade Center.
One woman's face caught my attention because she
looked something like me.

That night, in and out of sleep, I seemed to see
her sitting by my bed.

"Do I know you?" I asked.

She shook her head. "No. We've never met. But
my story could be yours, or yours mine."

"I know what you mean," I said. "I worked in New
York for a while, until I married and came West."

"I always hoped to live in the West someday."
She sighed.

We talked about our children, our grandchildren.
I told her that I was retired, that we traveled. She had
planned to retire in January, she said. "My husband
and I were to take a Caribbean cruise."

"I'm so sorry," I said.

Quietly she said, "September 11 was a beautiful morning. I got to my office in the World Trade center a little early, and picked up a phone to call my daughter. She's pregnant with her second. I heard the dial tone, then a loud roar."

She stopped talking.

Tears ached in my eyes, as they have so many times lately. I said, "That's all?"

"Yes," she said. "That's all. I was lucky. Many others died more painfully."

"Are you…staying around?" I asked. I had thought of the afterlife as more peaceful, more removed.

She shook her head. "Not long. But I have a message. There are things people must do."

"Anything," I said. "Send money?"

She nodded. "Yes, certainly, if you can. But that's not the most important thing."

She ticked off one finger. "First, pray. Pray for 'us' and pray for 'them.' Pray for our leaders and pray for theirs. Pray."

"Yes, of course."

"Second, stay in touch with everyone who is in your heart. Don't put off the call, the letter, the visit. Had I called a minute sooner my daughter would have heard my voice one last time — and I hers."

"All right," I managed to say.

"Third, fourth and fifth: keep healthy, keep cheerful and do your work."

Her image was fading. "Wait," I said. "Isn't there anything more we can do?"

I think she smiled. "Oh, I'm sure there will be, yes. But if people will do those things, then when

God's plan becomes clear they'll be able to help bring it about. Promise?"

"I promise," I said, and then she was gone.

Strengthen me God to use wisely my renewed awareness of life's fragility.

Fifty-six

Holy Day Resurrection

November 2001

You are my God; be gracious to me, O Lord,
for to you do I cry all day long.
Gladden the soul of your servant,
for to you, O Lord, I lift up my soul.– Psalm 86:2b-4

On the very top of our Christmas tree is a tiny gauze angel. Beneath that I always drape a short green and red construction paper chain with paste stains on it, made almost exactly thirty years ago. These two things are reminders of our own littlest angel, our son Tom, who drowned in 1971 at the age of three, only six months after making that paper chain. Each year I put these things on the tree in order to include him in family gatherings, and to remind myself that we will meet again some day. After all, every Holy Day in our calendar is about new life and resurrection. Tommy is the one who has gone ahead, who will be there to greet us when our times come.

His small everlasting light shows our family the way up from the deep darkness of sorrow.

Americans as a nation are in collective darkness. Much has changed in the few weeks since suicide planes destroyed the Twin Towers. We're worried, fearful, anxious, because something awful hides the light. Usually walls do that, but not this time. This time the light is hidden by the absence of walls, and by a wasteland of rubble and acrid smoke. We try to go back to the way things were before our national losses. We can't.

Living with personal grief can help teach us to live with national grief. It's a hard-won lesson. Every year there are people for whom the holiday season is an especially dark, sad, lonely time because a loved one no longer sits at the festive tables, no longer desires the presents we long to give them, no longer hangs ornaments on the tree. The recently bereaved manage to go on, for the sake of the other loved ones remaining here on earth. They know that when the way back is closed, God always provides a way forward, a way up and out, a way to new life. All we have to do is ask. All we have to do is seek. We have learned, through necessity, to look for resurrection everywhere.

This Christmas, in this country and other countries as well, thousands of people are experiencing that fresh grief because of the terrorist attacks. How may they, and we, cope? This is what I think we do: We pray for one another. We delight in even the briefest happiness. We turn our full attention on someone else's need. We gather together in love. We overlook small slights. We welcome all guests. We commit random acts of kindness. We take care of ourselves. We recall and retell our stories. We live within the beautiful moments. We laugh and sing, and relish life. So can joy and hope rise from despair to the top branches of the tree and the angels hovering there, and above that higher still to God.

Thank You God for those who have gone before and now light our way.

Fifty-seven

Advent Blue

December 2001

But Mary treasured all these words and pondered them in her heart. – Luke 2:19

One December, years ago, I noticed a woman in church who was weeping softly throughout the service. The second Sunday this happened, I took her aside and asked if we might help. "No," she said. "It's just that my brother died in July and this will be our first Christmas without him. In the streets it's so bright and cheery and noisy that I feel like a stranger. In here, it's softer. Here, it's okay to be sad."

This year our church has returned to the ancient practice of arraying the Advent altar with Marian blue—that is, with the color traditionally worn by Jesus' mother—instead of with the deeper, more penitential purple of Lent. The calm color seems to reflect the quiet solemnity of the group gathered around the manger that holds Mary's child. Whether family, Magi, shepherd, angel or beast, no one in that group laughs or shrieks with excitement the way TV families do on Christmas morning. All are quiet, worshipful. All, it seems, are pondering in their hearts what this wonderful thing could mean. For young Mary, with her God-given responsibility, the moment is especially portentous. Perhaps this first Christmas *gravitas* is the reason for the lack of connection between the world's frantic Christmas preparations and the church's quiet ones.

Yes it's okay to be sad, and not only in church. Sadness is one of our deepest textures as human beings. Even if we haven't lost someone recently, there's much to give us concern. For our world, ravaged and polluted. For our country, recently attacked and endangered. For our loved ones, scattered and out of our care. For ourselves, not so strong as we were nor so young.

Of course if we are hopelessly depressed for weeks on end, if our eating and sleeping habits have changed drastically, if our life and work is affected, we may need professional help. But most of us—if we don't rush to deny sadness, trying to eat or drink or spend it away—may learn through our sorrow important things about ourselves and our place in this life. Some of our most valuable ideas and decisions come when we're not all that happy.

God's promise this blue season is that one day the bright white and gold joy of Christmas will come for each of us. Not necessarily on December 25, but one day. One day soon...

Thank You God for my emotions this season, no matter what they are.

Fifty-eight

If Not Now, When?

January 2002

Happy are those who find wisdom,
and those who get understanding,
for her income is better than silver,
and her revenue better than gold. – Proverbs 3:13,14

It's January. At last, after the devastations of Fall 2001 and the distractions of the holidays, another year settles into its comforting rhythm of days, weeks, months, and seasons.

Yesterday I opened an Almanac, with its gardening tips, weather predictions, and wise sayings. You know the sayings I mean. Our mothers told them to us. When we were young we rejected them as outdated and trite. Now we can see their ancient truth.

Take: ***Don't put off until tomorrow what you can do today.***

"Like what, for instance."

Like that project, you know the one. The stitchery picture for the nursery wall to be finished while the baby's still little. The story from childhood that's begging to be told or written down. The still-empty bins bought to organize the storage room. The exercise program at the Natatorium, starting this month.

The Adult Ed class at Skyline School to take, or to teach, next quarter.

"I've begun things before, and given up on them."

Start anyway. Maybe this beginning will be different. *Well begun is half done.*

"But I have no time."

Maybe not. But probably there's an hour or two somewhere. *You have all the time there is.*

"Why should I start anything, when the world is so unsettled?"

But that's exactly why. The worst thing we can do now is become frazzled and distracted, unable to focus and concentrate. Our work benefits everyone. Whatever makes us more whole and complete pleases God and almost invariably connects us with other people. Pursuing our talents and interests puts us in touch with family, with dear friends, with strangers whose interests are the same. *Do your best and be your best and you'll be happy.*

"Must I start right now? Can't it wait a while?"

Can it? *There's no time like the present.*

"Yes, but I'm still feeling so anxious..."

Of course. What better reason to busy our hands and our minds? The most important lesson we've lately learned is that time is not infinite.

If not now, when?
If not I, who?

Thank You God for the sage messages from my past.

Fifty-nine

The Sacrament of Affirmation

February 2002

Let love be genuine; hate what is evil, hold fast to what is good; love one another with mutual affection; outdo one another in showing honor. – Romans 12:9,10

Happy Valentines, Miss Jones
You sure have nice bones!

The small boy (on the PBS show "Sesame Street," I think) who spontaneously came up with this couplet was embarrassed because his admiration for his teacher had exceeded his poetic ability. Fortunately his teacher also possessed a good heart. Puzzled but grateful, she warmly thanked the boy for the sentiment. She recognized that the poem was a genuine compliment.

When I was in Junior High in Indiana, there was a short-lived fad of sending cruel, anonymous Valentine cards. A gentle English teacher I'll call Mrs. Austin, whose love for her subject was obvious and contagious, received a couple of "Mean, Ugly Old Teacher" cards one year. I didn't know who sent them, but I had heard they were sent. That day, someone reported, in hushed tones, that they had seen Mrs. Austin crying at her desk. That Spring she took early retirement. We heard that she had lost heart because of the so-called "Valentines." We were surprised. Children often forgot that teachers are human, too.

Was Mrs. Austin over-sensitive? Perhaps. But I, for one, have never forgotten her, because she was an early example for me of how words can hurt us, and hurt us deeply.

On the other hand, the right words allow us to flourish.

Who can say those right words? You and I. While only Bishops administer the Sacrament of Confirmation, each of us is empowered to administer the Sacrament of Affirmation—at any time and to anyone. We do that by telling the person why he or she is valued by us. There's only one rule: *the praise must be sincere*. True compliments are hard enough to accept. False ones are dismissed out of hand.

How many people are gone from your life for whose loving presence you will always be grateful? I know I can think of several just off the top of my head. Do you sometimes wish you had told them so, or told them so more often? I know I do.

Here's a Valentine-month suggestion. In remembrance of our loved ones now gone, and in celebration of those still with us, let's turn our Valentine thoughts and words to four or five of the people who make a difference to us right now. Maybe there's someone whose smile brightens our day, someone whose sense of humor lightens our mood, someone whose thoughtfulness is out of the ordinary. (Or someone who has nice bones.) If giving a compliment is too hard to do face to face, we can send the person a note.

He or she will inevitably take heart and be made stronger by the blessing of our words.

Strengthen me God to thank those who have had a positive influence on my life.

Sixty

Confession

March 2002

We have done those things which we ought not to have done, and left undone those things which we ought to have done, and there is no health in us.
— *The 1928 Book of Common Prayer General Confession*

Last night, after the Lenten soup supper, I came home and ate a chocolate from my Valentine box. Then I thought, *I ought not to have done that. It not Lenten, and it's not healthy.*

The above words from an old Confession stay with many of us, and not only because of their beauty and cadence. They stay with us because they express how we feel about ourselves all too often.

I'm the last person to advocate a return to an earlier prayer book with its relentlessly male wording. Certainly "what we have done and what we have left undone," in the Confession we now say, covers the ground just as well.

But there's something about those older words...

A recent study shows that what we feel most guilty about is eating the wrong foods while avoiding the right foods. As sins go, that one seems unimportant, though it may fit under Greed. But if what we eat matters so much to so many of us, it can't be all that trivial.

So let's ask why we feel as we do. For one thing, we know that poor eating leads to poor health, the physical kind as well as the spiritual kind referred to in the Confession. Secondly, we know we look our best when we eat the right things. Thirdly, we realize that what we eat is under our control. We are capable of taking the salad not the burger, the fruit not the caramel. So why, we ask ourselves, don't we do it more often? *What's wrong with me?*

Bottom line, our diet is important to our feelings of worthiness. Luckily, Lent provides the perfect framework for trying to do better. Many religions have dietary restrictions such as our Lenten ones. Partly this is done to distinguish the faithful from the non-believers, and partly to keep people from eating foods that make them sick. Besides, discipline in food and drink can lead to discipline in other ways. Cutting down on unneeded fats and sugars can give us the strength and the will to cut other inessentials out of our lives, to cut to the core of what matters: love, health, family, friendship, and living in God's ways. If lapsing from a diet makes us feel bad, sticking to it raises our spirits and our good feelings about ourselves.

A few weeks are left in Lent. There's still time to leave the butter off the roll, to order the salad not the burger, to choose the apple over the chocolate.

We do it for God and for ourselves, and when we do, we feel a whole lot better.

Strengthen me God to make the right choices in my diet.

Sixty-one

You are There

April 2002

Where can I go from your spirit?
Or where can I flee from your presence?
If I ascend to heaven, you are there;
if I make my bed in Sheol, you are there.
If I take the wings of the morning
and settle at the farthest limits of the sea,
even there your hand shall lead me,
and your right hand shall hold me fast.
- Psalm 139:7-10

    I finished praying my imperfectly memorized version of these verses and opened my eyes. Nothing had changed. The noisy little Horizons plane was still bumping through the air in sickening lurches. The young Asian man sitting beside me in the other bulkhead seat was still white-knuckling the armrests. I couldn't see my friends, seated behind me. It didn't help that the time was 1 a.m., and that Martha, Patti and I were exhausted after waiting all day in the Seattle airport through mysterious flight cancellations and equipment failures. It didn't help that this was the same aircraft whose equipment had been unusable only a few hours earlier. I stared at the closed, locked cabin door and worried. *Did they know what they were doing in there? Were they all right?*

But then my gaze fell on the pretty flight attendant seated only a few feet away, facing us. She looked back at me with her serene, dark-lashed blue eyes and she smiled. Immediately I felt reassured. *Even there your hand will lead me.*

Two days later, rested and with the scary ride almost forgotten, I sat in a hospital room with our son Matthew watching our newest grandson nurse as he gazed into his mother's face. The thought came to me that birth and those first weeks out of the womb must be a lot like a bumpy, noisy plane ride through space, sending the newborn from comfortable, quiet security to light and noise and quick movement. It wasn't only calories little Ashton was receiving from Korie, but comfort and consolation too.

Surely God means for us to reassure one another of God's saving presence among us. In times of fear and uncertainty, we gaze on the faces of parents, friends, husbands, wives, flight attendants, or whatever authority figures may be around, silently asking *Is it okay? Are you okay? Am I?* Often we find the reassurance we need. The best way we can show our gratitude is to be reassuring when others gaze at us. We needn't even feel all that confident in the situation. All we need do is remember the strength and presence of God, and we too can smile serenely.

Thank You God for people who convey to me Your reassuring Presence.

Sixty-two

Good Job, Self!

May 2002

And now, Father, send us out to do the work you have given us to do, to love and serve you as faithful witnesses of Christ our Lord. – Book of Common Prayer, p. 366

Listen to your inner dialog to yourself, about yourself. Is it mostly affirming or mostly disparaging? Is it, *Nice work*! Or is it *How could I be so stupid?*

Which kind of inner dialog allows us to do God's work more fully and enthusiastically? Self-affirmation does. As I wrote in an earlier letter, the affirming of others can be a sacrament. Well, so can affirming ourselves. But because we were taught not to be conceited, because we took to heart the criticisms we received when we were young, because we've not been able to accomplish all we hoped we would, we tend to get down on ourselves.

This last weekend I spent in Boulder, Colorado, at a Refresher Workshop for <u>Guideposts</u> writers. We were discussing one of the submitted stories, which had to do with the overcoming of failure. The point of these workshops is to offer constructive criticism, and the editors who lead them are very good at doing this, as are many of the other writers. In attempt to suggest how the story might be made more vivid, the

Articles Editor said to the story's author, whom I'll call Dolores, "Have you ever failed at anything?"

Tears came to Dolores's eyes. "My life is nothing but failure," she whispered.

All of us, including the editor, were taken aback by her reaction.

Now, Dolores is a beautiful person both inside and out. She is a terrific wife and mother, and a successful writer whose name is on the masthead of the most-read inspirational magazine in the world. Yet she felt that bad about herself.

As other Workshoppers began showering Dolores with compliments, she kept her eyes down and muttered, "Thank you," to each. But I don't think she even heard them. Somewhere along the line, someone had shaken her confidence too badly for her ever to recover completely.

Eventually another Workshopper said, "What we call failure is really God's re-direction of our lives." We agreed, and Dolores said, "Thanks, that helps," and objectivity was restored to the meeting.

But the incident made me realize that much of the time we are too hard on ourselves. We need to feel good about the things we do. It helps if we can see our accomplished work as God's doing as well as ours, as God moving through us, guiding our hands and steps. After all, God's good work is done through God's people. Through me. Through you.

Good job, self, and thanks, God!

Thank You God for my accomplishments, granted and guided by You.

Sixty-three

Living a Dog's Life

June 2002

This is the day that the Lord has made; let us rejoice and be glad in it. - *Psalm 118:24*

Currently at our house, which we've shared for the past thirteen years with a small, enthusiastic terrier-mix named Clare, we're laughing over an anonymous internet mailing called, "A Dog's Diary." It goes something like this:

Thursday, June 6
OH BOY! MORNING! MY FAVORITE!
OH BOY! MOM! MY FAVORITE!
OH BOY! DOG FOOD! MY FAVORITE!
OH BOY! A WALK! MY FAVORITE!
OH BOY! RAIN! MY FAVORITE!
OH BOY! A CAR RIDE! MY FAVORITE!
OH BOY! A NAP! MY FAVORITE!
OH BOY! A WALK! MY FAVORITE!
OH BOY! SUNSHINE! MY FAVORITE!
OH BOY! A SQUIRREL! MY FAVORITE!
OH BOY! ROTTING GARBAGE! MY FAVORITE!
(Bath. Bummer.)
OH BOY! DAD! MY FAVORITE!

OH BOY! A BONE! MY FAVORITE!
OH BOY! NIGHTTIME! MY FAVORITE!

Friday, June 7
OH BOY! MORNING! MY FAVORITE!
OH BOY! MOM! MY FAVORITE!
OH BOY! DOG FOOD! MY FAVORITE!

And so on.

I think this anonymous dog, and our dog, and all the dogs I know have captured the secret meaning of life. No need to travel to a mountaintop in India and find a guru to ask. Consult the nearest dog. If you don't know one, feel free to come over and visit mine.

Oh come on, you say. *What, run around acting foolishly happy with all the duties and responsibilities and troubles that I have? Get real.*

Okay, it's true our lives are more complicated and worrisome than those of companion animals. But still we are given only so many moments of life to enjoy. At countless times throughout the day, when we have completed a task or when we can take a break from one, let's not begin immediately fretting about the next task. Let's stop, and rejoice, and be glad for every beautiful detail of our world and our place in it.

Take June. Take the season when we can enjoy the incredible green of the grass, the cool taste of melon, the bright chirp of a bird, a whiff of a yellow flower, the long blue light of evening. Take June, to stop, draw a deep breath, and thank God for the goodness of creation. Take June—it's yours.

If we live this way, our diary may read:

Sunday, June 9
OH BOY! MORNING! MY FAVORITE!
OH BOY! A WARM SHOWER! MY FAVORITE!
OH BOY! BREAKFAST! MY FAVORITE!
OH BOY! CHURCH! MY FAVORITE!

Thank You God for every thing that lifts my spirits.

Sixty-four

For Those in Peril on the Sea
July 2002

Oh, hear us when we cry to Thee for those in peril on the sea. – Hymnal 579, words by William Whiting

The words of the hymn came to my mind last month as our 197-foot windjammer sailing ship sped among the volcanic Caribbean islands known as the Grenadines. Storm clouds gathered in the east. White-capped waves rocked us, sometimes splashing into the lower deck where we were sitting. In order to move around safely, we clung to a network of ropes over our heads, hands meeting hands.

Eventually I'd had enough, so I made my way to our comfortable cabin. There I lay on my bunk, turned on the bed light and read a novel, judiciously postponing my shower until things were quieter.

By mealtime, the wind and water had calmed. The sails came down, the engine came on, the ship slowed, and we ate a delicious buffet meal on the upper deck as we gazed at the incredible blue-green of the sea.

We were never in any real physical peril. Not the kind of peril my ancestors—perhaps yours too—faced when they made the voyage from England in the 1600's on ships half the size of that windjammer.

Our ancestors had no comfortable cabins or auxiliary engines or showers or buffet meals. Their trips lasted not one week, but as many as twelve. Conditions were unpleasant to say the least, as they shared their quarters with shifting property and smelly livestock, eating hard bread and salty meat, drinking barreled water that turned nasty as time went on. Often they were cold and wet. Yet only one ship sank of the 198 that sailed during the 1630's, and the mortality rate from disease was less than 5 percent. God was merciful.

Why did the early colonists endure all that? Because they preferred the physical dangers of the sea to the worldly dangers in an England that for them held economic and spiritual inequality, heedless violence and rampant materialism.

Yes, the church from which they separated was our parent Anglican church. But that dictatorial, royalty-ridden, 17th Century institution can hardly be compared to our beleaguered and dwindling Episcopal denomination. We are divided from within as well as besieged from without by the same worldly dangers and hatreds that our ancestors feared. Still we, like they, are connected by the strong ropes of compassion and truth, hands meeting hands. If we can hang on together, by God's mercy, we too can weather any storm.

Strengthen me God to connect with those who weather the storms of life with me.

Sixty-five

"I Meant To Do My Work Today"
August, 2002

I went down to the nut orchard, to look at the blossoms of the valley, to see whether the vines had budded, whether the pomegranates were in bloom.
– *Song of Solomon, 6:11*

"*I meant to do my work today,*" wrote the poet Richard Le Galienne. But butterflies and blowing leaves were too much for him. He took a side trip, just as the writer of the Song of Solomon did. Why? Just because.

Don't we say that too, sometimes? "I meant to do my work today." But usually we say it ruefully, guiltily. Why? What's so important, after all?

Recently I met a retired person who said, "I took my work too seriously all those years. Now I can't think why. I'd have done it just as well if I'd relaxed and enjoyed myself a little. Everyone would have been better off."

It's August, when the world draws a deep breath, makes new priorities, thinks long lazy thoughts, leans back and sighs. Remember last August, the month before all hell broke loose on 9/11? Remember the heedless days we had then—a long vacation, a weekend camping trip, a family reunion? Remember the time away, when work could be forgotten?

Some would say last August happened eons ago in American social history. But in God's history, little has changed. The earth has turned once more, that's all. It's deep summer again, and the birds and butterflies, grasses, wind and rainbows are still where they've always been. If what happened in September can keep us mindful of the earth's wonder and sweetness, then at least one good thing has come of it.

We've just returned from a time with ten friends and relatives at our old log cabin on the Rocky Mountain Front. We slung our hammock between two trees and, one after another or two at a time, lay there and read. It was wonderful.

Here are quotations on this same theme from a couple of other writers:

William Shakespeare*: "Summer's lease hath all too short a date."* George MacDonald: *"Work is not always required...there is such a thing as sacred idleness, the cultivation of which is now fearfully neglected."*

Isn't there a book or two you've been meaning to read? A hammock or its equivalent that has your name on it?

Now's the time.

Thank You God for long summer days.

Sixty-six

Frances

September 2004

Every generous act of giving, with every perfect gift, is from above… - James 1:17a

Once again it's my birthday month. These days it's better to recall the wonderful gifts of the past than to ask for new ones. Just now I'm regarding a doll I received on my fifth Christmas, when we lived for a few months in Los Angeles near my paternal grandparents' home. Frances is a gently contoured little-girl doll, thirteen inches tall, an Effanbee. She has a cap of waved, honey hair that is only slightly mussed.

When I came into the living room that Christmas morning the adults all looked at me expectantly. There, hanging from the tree, magical and misty in pink tulle, was this doll. I was awe-struck.

"Is she mine?" I asked. Gentle laughter came from all the adults, even from Grandfather Roberts who was a gray, distant, scolding man as a rule.

"Yes dear. It's a present from Grandfather. Thank Grandfather."

"Thank you, Grandfather."

"You are welcome, Caroline."

Frances came with the dress she floated in and one or two more. But also in her red cardboard suitcase (which I still have) were other clothes. These were the clothes my mother had made, night after night, while I was in bed. They were mostly hand-sewn, with tiny stitches and delicate trim. The outfit Frances wears today is a blue elastic-waisted pinafore with pink roses, a white dotted-Swiss blouse, and a pair of ribbon-trimmed panties.

She had many many other clothes too—green slacks and a yellow blouse, a cream-colored night-gown trimmed in red, school clothes, party clothes, play clothes, even coats. Some I still have.

Frances herself was deadpan and poky-hard, impossible to sleep with (though I tried). Awake and in her clothes, though, she was me. Not as I was, incompetent and clumsy, but as I meant to be—clever, helpful and brave.

Adults who came across me as I played with Frances, my lips moving in dialogue, would say, "Wasn't it nice of your grandfather to give you such a pretty doll?" Head down, I would nod. And so it was. Nice of him. She may even have been his idea, though it's hard to believe he would have concerned himself for even a moment with something so trivial.

No, Frances' true value to me came through my mother's love and skill, through the clothes that brought her to life and made her not only mine, but me.

So for Frances then and Frances now, while I do thank my grandfather, I thank my mother more.

Thank You God for all the love-enhanced gifts I have received through the years.

Sixty-seven

Changing Time

October 2002

All the works of the Lord are very good, and what-
ever he commands will be done at the appointed time.
— *Sirach, 39:16*

We'll soon be going off Daylight Saving Time. They tell us we're gaining an hour because we get to do 2 a.m. to 3 a.m. twice. Or is it 1 a.m. to 2 a.m.? Whichever it is doesn't feel like time gained, no matter what they say. Like flying in a plane across time zones, going on or off Daylight Saving Time is tiring and disorienting. It also means we have to change all the timekeepers around us, which in my case happen to number about fifteen. Some change themselves automatically, as the computer and cable TV. *(How do they know?)* On the other end of the difficulty scale are the car clocks, for which I always have to consult the book.

In order to go off daylight saving, we have to pay attention to time. We have to move it around in the way we are told. We have no choice. It's out of our control. So while we're at it, why not pay attention to other time-changing in our lives where we do have control? Maybe we could really gain time where it counts—or spend time where it counts.

For example, if we always take an efficient shower, we can take a long, soaking bath. Our sense of well-being may be enhanced. Or if baths are our norm, we can do the shower and since they're usually faster, we'll have time to read interesting stories in the Great Falls Tribune through to the end

A couple of other suggestions: If we are all business when we phone, even when we phone friends, we can take some time to chat. After all, the business world makes us wait and wait while we punch numbers and listen to music-like sounds. Isn't it better to spend extra phone time with a friend? On the other hand, if our habit is to gab on and on for no particular reason, a timer could be freeing.

If we watch a lot of TV, a television-free day every week can add unbelievable space to our lives—space for writing letters, practicing an instrument, walking around a park, reading a new book, just plain thinking. On the other hand if we watch no TV at all, we could try a channel or two: CSpan. The Learning Channel(TLC). Discovery. History. PBS. It's possible to learn much from good TV.

The point is to take charge of an aspect or two of our lives. Why? Because we can. Because our souls may gain by it. Because it feels good.

Thank You God for the hours that are under my control.

Sixty-eight

"I Sing a Song of the Saints of God"
November 2002

I sing a song of the saints of God, patient and brave and true,
who toiled and fought and lived and died for the Lord they loved and knew.
And one was a doctor, and one was a queen, and one was a shepherdess on the green:
they were all of them saints of God and I mean, God helping, to be one too.

- Hymnal 293, words by Lesbia Scott

It's November, the month of saints. On All Saints Day, November 1, we think of the saints and faithful departed who have gone before. For the rest of the month, let's think of the saints still around us.

Last month we took a week-long Caribbean cruise. On Wednesday, we disembarked and rode on an air-conditioned bus through the hot, lush Yucatan countryside to visit Mayan ruins. From the tinted bus windows we saw poor Mexican villages consisting of a few dozen ramshackle houses, a small stucco church with open bell tower, tiny shops, and palm-covered shelters advertising cold drinks. We saw schoolyards with uniformed children playing games, and dirt lanes with people walking in twos and threes. Often they waved and we waved back.

By evening we were sitting on our ship's cabin balconies, relaxing before a sumptuous meal and watching the cerulean blue of the Caribbean flow by.

The contrast between the villagers' lives and ours was striking and disturbing—and should be. We middle-class U.S. Americans are indeed privileged. Some would say that our very privilege excludes us from God's presence, and certainly from saintliness.

But this is a defeatist way to look at things, since so very few of us are going to give away everything to work among the poor, or would be particularly effective if we did.

It's my belief that there are saints among the villagers in Yucatan, and saints among the passengers and crew of the Grand Princess, and saints in Great Falls, some of whom attend church at Incarnation. We are who we are, in our own place and time, and our goal should be to live our lives the best way we know how. I think that the saints are those in every society who believe what they practice and practice what they believe. Who touch and help others in profound ways by fully being who they are, and by remembering their obligation to God and neighbor. Who not only talk and worry about inequality and injustice but try to find ways to bring about a better world.

We all know some of these people. November is a good time to think on them, to thank God for them, to work toward being like them.

Strengthen me God to become the saint that You mean me to be.

Sixty-nine

A Brighter Place

December 2002

For everything there is a season,
and a time for every matter under heaven:
a time to be born, and a time to die….
– Ecclesiastes 3:1-2a

My lady mother Blanche Wylie Roberts, aged 100, died on November 18. I was in the room with her as she quietly departed this life with as much grace, consideration and dignity as she had lived it.

People often exclaim over all the changes those of my mother's generation have seen. They are speaking of such things as the electrification of rural America, the widespread use of automobiles, world wars, air travel, telecommunications, movies, radio, television, computers. But these things were not bewildering or disorienting to people like Mother, because the basics did not change: Family. Friendship. Faith. She stayed grounded in these things. Through everything, she stayed cheerful. So many of you have remarked that you will miss Mother's delighted laugh, her radiant smile. As will I, every day.

At the end, I believe Mother knew her time had come. A few years ago her son-in-law Bill said, "Blanche, you need to live to be a hundred." And so she did. We think that she determined to stay alive for the big birthday party and family reunion we had in Missoula in August, because it was after that, after seeing her surviving brother and sister, that she began to fail.

The November 22 Great Falls <u>Tribune</u> that printed her obituary also carried this item in L.M. Boyd's column:

"What's the most common cause of death for people over 100?"

"No one disease...Belief is most centenarians purposefully set target times, then simply shut down the bodily machinery as planned. They will themselves to die exactly as they'd willed themselves to live."

To us, this seemed to be what happened with Mother.

I was privileged to keep vigil with Mother in her room at Beehive Homes, Missoula, under Hospice comfort care, the last three days of her life. On Friday, together with the visiting chaplain, I prayed, as I have done at the bedside of so many parishioners, the Prayer Book's "Commendation at the Time of Death." On Saturday, even though Mother had ceased talking, she gave my sister and me her last lovely, unmatchable smile. On Monday, her breathing ceased.

While Mother was not a poet, she loved words, and when she had occasion to speak profoundly she did. I've always remembered what she wrote me when her own mother died at the age of 95. I've remembered, but never really understood until what she meant until it happened to me.

Mother wrote, "The world is not so bright a place without my mother in it."

It's true for me too now. The world has dimmed a little. But it's true as well, I do believe, that Heaven is now a little brighter.

Thank You God for my mother.

Seventy

Epiphany

January 2003

O God, by the leading of a star you manifested your only Son to the peoples of the earth: Lead us, who know you now by faith, to your presence, where we may see your glory face to face... The Book of Common Prayer, p. 214

At least since the 1950s, maybe earlier, my parents, sisters and I had a table-top Nativity set with a rustic stable and small plaster figures. At the Woolworths of the time, items for sale weren't encased in plastic but were available for handing. The Christmas figurines

198

were placed loose in small bins. The shopper chose kings, a Mary, a donkey, and so on, paying maybe a quarter for each.

For many years our set was complete. But in 1967, when Father retired from teaching Political Science at Wabash College in Indiana, my parents moved across the country to Sonoma, California, and many things were lost. When Father died in 1989, Mother moved a few times on her own, and more things were lost. The Nativity set shrank. The stable and several figures were lost. In December 2001, there were only seven Nativity items sitting on our piano: Mary, Joseph, a king, an angel, a donkey, a camel, and a sheep.

Not enough to tell the story.

So for the Christmas of 2002, I searched on *ebay*, an auction web site, and found a set to fill in. Now there's a stable that's grander than the one we used to have, and added to the original figures are another donkey, a cow, two kings, two shepherds, and a Baby Jesus.

There's no way to tell where any of the figures were manufactured. The newer ones were probably not made in this country, but in a sunnier place. I conclude this because the humans are darker-skinned, and are actually more authentic for the Middle Eastern Biblical climate.

I love looking at the combined set. It reminds me of what Epiphany is all about: the mingling of the old and the new, the family joined by strangers who then become friends. It reminds me that the only way to a lasting peace is for people to come together in understanding and acceptance.

Probably none of us plans to visit the Holy Land soon. The times are too frightening. But that doesn't mean Bethlehem can't be in our hearts—or on our pianos. Whenever people come together in common purpose that works toward justice, hope, affection and humility, don't we have a small Bethlehem right there?

Thank You God for those strangers who have touched me and been touched by me.

Seventy-one

Many Rooms

April 2003

In my Father's house there are many dwelling places. If it were not so, would I have told you that I go to prepare a place for you? – John 14:2

Like many other Americans, Ben and Allie were competitive people. They were competitive on their jobs and in their lifestyle and in sports and games. Not only were they competitive, they often came out ahead. They believed that winners beget winners, and when little Myra was born they were quick to point out that she walked and talked much sooner than did the children of their friends.

Unfortunately they didn't realize how their competitiveness sounded to the sensitive child.

Allie would say, "I beat Jennifer out of that assignment this morning. Left her in the dust."

Ben would exult, "You should have seen Harold's face at the quota meeting when I announced my new clients! A year from now I'll have his job and he'll be gone."

Then Allie got pregnant again. When they told the happy news to Myra, now four, the little girl got a sick feeling in her stomach. One evening she overheard her parents talking: "When the new baby is in Myra's room…"

So. Her worst fears were realized. She was to be left in the dust, gone, and soon. The little girl's heart sank and her stomach ached. She went to her room, pulled out her canvas tote bag, and packed it with socks, underwear, a favorite teddy bear, her toothbrush.

Luckily Allie caught sight of Myra as she was opening the front door. "Honey, where are you going?"

"I'm making room for the baby," she said in a quavering voice. "Goodbye."

After a moment of stunned disbelief, Allie scooped the child into her arms, held her tightly and carried her down the hall to the seldom-used guest room.

"This was to be a surprise," Allie said. "But you need to see it now." She threw open the door.

Myra gasped and her eyes got big. The room was right out of a story book, with its ruffled yellow bed cover and canopy, its yellow-flowered wallpaper. "It's yours, honey," Allie said, with tears in her eyes. "We fixed it up in your favorite color. The baby will sleep in your old room."

Myra clung to her mother and wept with relief. Through her own tears, Allie said gently, "You know you'll have a room near Daddy and me for as long as you want one. And you'll always be in our hearts, always and forever. We love you so much!"

"But what about the new baby?"

"Of course we'll love the new baby too. It doesn't mean we love you less. Moms and dads have places in their hearts for all of their children."

Myra's own heart swelled with joy.

After that incident, Allie and Ben become more aware of how competitive they sounded. As their girl and boy grew, they tried very hard not to make comparisons that would pit one against the other, or either against their peers. They also found their own goals changing, and winning became less important to them than spending family time together.

Eventually they moved to a smaller house. But the room in Ben's and Allie's hearts only grew larger.

That's how it is with God. God's great heart has room and place for us all, always, no matter how many of us are living there. Jesus told us so.

Thank You God for all the children dwelling in my heart.

Seventy-two

Little Dog Clare
1988 – 2003
May 2003

Weeping may linger for the night,
but joy comes with the morning. – *Psalm 30:5b*

Our little dog Clare was sweet and spoiled, a lover and a beggar, and to every day and every person in her life she said, *Yes! Yes! Yes!*

But she'd been slowing down for months. She had stopped jumping up, she couldn't hear well, and she slept a lot. That Monday she was clearly in trouble, could barely move. The veterinarian, Dr. G, did some blood tests and sent her home. But Tuesday and Tuesday night he kept her, hoping IV's would build up her blood pressure enough so that medication could be tried. I hoped, and I prayed.

On Wednesday morning, the vet called to say that Clare hadn't improved and that while she wasn't in pain now, she would be soon. Bill went with me to the vet clinic and we stayed while Dr. G's euthanized Clare. That way I could stroke her, and ours could be the last faces she saw before she died.

I was a wreck that day—too distraught to go to Bible study or the noon service. People were kind and thoughtful, calling and sending cards and flowers to let me know they understood.

Clare was 15 when she died. She was my first dog after many cats. Over the years, daughter Sarah had developed an allergy to cats, and they weren't an option for us as permanent pets. But I did miss having an animal around, so 14 years ago I drove out to the Humane Society Shelter to look at the dogs.

When I came to the little black and tan dog in Run #29, she leaped for joy to see me, as though she'd been waiting. She was a terrier mix, they said, left there by her original family for chewing the children's toys. Their loss was our gain. When I picked her up, she laid her long black nose in the hollow of my neck. From that moment she was mine. There hasn't been a day or night since when I didn't have Clare's whereabouts and care on my mind. I always knew where she was and how she was doing.

I believe that right now she's doing fine.

If our lives in eternity are related to the fullness, the love, and the authenticity of our lives here on earth—and I feel that they are—then companion animals have surely earned their place in heaven. I like to think that Clare is with her old friend my mother, both of them as young as they want to be. I like to think that Clare will be in the group that meets me when I go there too

What a joyful day that will be!

Thank You God for the companion animals of my life.

Seventy-three

Visiting the Sick and the Housebound
March 2003

Then the king will say to those at his right hand, "Come, you that are blessed by my Father, inherit the kingdom prepared for you from the foundation of the world; for...I was sick and you took care of me"...And the king will answer them, "Truly I tell you, just as you did it to one of the least of these who are members of my family, you did it to me."
— Matthew 25:34,36,40

People sometimes ask me about visiting the sick, since they know I do this regularly as part of my Deacon ministry. They may say:

I know I should visit my old friend in the nursing home, but I can't find the time.
Everyone is endowed with all the time there is, and hospital, nursing home or home visiting doesn't have to take a big chunk of it. Just sitting with someone half an hour can make a big difference to both of you.

But what do we talk about?
If this concerns you, bring along something to read aloud that has caught your interest. But the best prep-

aration is consciously to clear your mind of your own troubles and worries. What would concern you if you were in the sick person's place? Start with a quiet, non-intrusive question. Be ready to listen. Listening is what it's all about.

Do I just show up?

If you're visiting in a hospital or nursing home, yes, that's fine. If the person is in their own home, call first. Mid-morning and mid-afternoon are usually best.

I don't know. My life is complicated enough as it is. Someday maybe, when I'm less busy.

Okay, but first read what people have said about visiting the sick. (The names have been changed):

"It makes me feel good, because people are usually so welcoming and glad to talk. It takes me out of myself for a while." *Ben, 72, retired accountant*

"I go because people visited me when I broke my leg, and I was always happy to see them. I remember every person who came, and that was ten years ago!" *Elizabeth, 38, real estate agent*

"Well, it's the right thing to do, isn't it? Maybe that sounds pious. Anyway, I know I feel better about how I use my free time if I visit with someone and not just play a computer game or watch TV." *Jeremy, 19, student*

"A friend from work without a church family never got visited the whole time her little girl was so sick. I didn't want that to happen to me. So that's what got me up and going. Now I go because I like to." *Libby, 45, office manager*

Can't I just make phone call?
Phone calls are good too, but less personal. Nothing is better than the warmth of a comforting presence by one's side.

Try it. Try it once. See how good you'll feel.

Strengthen me God to visit the sick and find You there.

Seventy-four

No Return

June 2003

And remember, I am with you always, to the end of the age. - Matthew 28:20b

Between Helena and Great Falls, between the mountains and the plains, there's an isolated stretch of highway with no signs of civilization in sight. There is only an exit that appears to head off into nowhere. The sign for it reads: *NO RETURN TO I-15 NORTH*

That sign gives me a shiver of anxiety. It seems to say: "*Make this move and there's no going back. Swerve here, and your life is forever altered in ways you cannot know.*"

I've never used that exit, but over the years my life has taken many turns that meant exactly that. *This is it. No going back.* Yours has too, I'm sure.

Sometimes the words announcing change are welcome:

"*You have been accepted into the program.*"

"*Yes, of course I'll marry you!*"

"*Your pregnancy test is positive.*"

"*Congratulations! The job is yours.*"

But as desirable as a new path may seem, choosing to take it almost always causes anxiety. We all have a fear of the unknown. We all sometimes long to keep to the familiar way. Once certain exits are chosen, there can be no return. A recent trip to Indiana for a high school reunion reminded me of that. Yes, we old friends met, hugged, reminisced. But never again would we gather at a sleep-over to plan and hope and dream together. We had our own families and friends now. We had settled deeply into our separate lives. Besides that, the world we knew had changed beyond any of our reckoning. No return. Not ever.

Sadly, sometimes the life-turning words cause our hearts to fail us:

"We're downsizing and have to let you go. I'm sorry."

"The lab results aren't good."

"I've found someone else and I want a divorce."

"There's been an accident."

Then our new road seems more than obscure, it seems impassable.

But we believers are luckier than other people, because our Way is never blocked for long. Although the unknown road may seem desolate and isolated, with no destination in sight, we know we need not fear. We know that God is good, that God has a plan for every life, unclear as that plan may be on any given day. We know that God would never leave us to journey on alone. With God there always is a return to where we ought to be.

Thank You God for the crucial turnings of my life.

Seventy-five

Take a Moment...

August 2003

It is good to give thanks to the Lord,
to sing praises to your name, O Most High;
to declare your steadfast love in the morning,
and your faithfulness by night,
to the music of the lute and harp,
to the melody of the lyre.
For you, O Lord, have made me glad by your work;
at the works of your hands I sing for joy.
— Psalm 92:1-4

It's not quite 8 a.m. on a summer Saturday. I sit in a green-padded chair on the deck of the house where we've lived for almost 29 years. Mother's sweet-natured calico cat Kristy lies in a graceful curve on my lap.

A breeze occasionally stirs the leaves on the tree between me and the pale golden field beyond the chain link fence. The deck is shaded at this time of day, but the morning sun shines on the dewy corn stalks and red raspberries in our garden. A squirrel ripples up the tree, down again, is gone. I know that Kristy wouldn't care about the squirrel any more than she does about the birds on the lawn, even if she were awake. Her hunting days are over. I like that in a cat.

A few thin clouds lie over the Highwood Mountains away to the south; other than that, the sky is a soft, uniform blue. Under the tree, the still water in the bird bath reflects the leaved branch hanging above it. In the rock garden that stretches the length of the back yard, the tall white and gold daisies of midsummer sway and shine.

From the CD player inside comes the second movement of Beethoven's Violin Concerto. The only other sounds are the lazy chirp of birds and the distant rumble of cars on Tenth Avenue South.

In my mind, my mother, who would have been 101 this month but who in November was freed from the weight of her years, sits quietly in the other green chair beside me and says, *What a lovely morning!* In my mind I say, *Yes*. Then I say, *Do you need anything, Mother? A sweater, something to drink?*

No, she says, as she used to say so often, *I don't need a thing*.

Nor do I. All that I need, by the grace of God, I have. Troubles have come, troubles will come again, but right now, right here, everything is fine.

This long summer moment is mine and mine only. I take it, cherish it, and thank God for it. You can find such moments too, no matter how busy your life may be. When you do find one, take it. Keep it. Hold it in your heart.

Thank You God for remembered sweet moments.

Seventy-six

Close Call

September 2003

Blessed be the Lord, for he has heard the sound of my pleadings. - *Psalm 28:6*

One day last week I had a close call. Downtown, driving east, I turned left from Central onto Sixth Street North as soon as the light turned green. I knew no pedestrians were stepping off the curb. But suddenly, right in front of me in the cross walk, was a woman who had started walking across from the other direction on the red light.

My brakes caught and held. The woman frowned at me as she reached the sidewalk and I gave her a weak "sorry" smile. Badly shaken, I parked. "Thank you, God," I prayed. "From now on I'll be more careful."

So close! Another second or two, and her life and mine would have been changed forever.

Maybe you've never had a close call like this—the classic "where did that car/person/dog/deer come from?" Eventually, if we live long enough and drive long enough, most of us do. Usually nothing bad happens, and we thank God.

But sometimes a close call will go the other way. The foot hits the gas not the brake. The stop sign gets lost in the sun. The bee, the spilled drink, the ringing cell phone distracts us at just the wrong time. Then health is lost, or a life, or more than one life. What do we do then? How do we pray when the bad thing has happened?

Repetitive prayer is almost instinctive when times are toughest, as we call on God and beg for help. Then there are the prayers people have relied on for centuries: The 23rd Psalm. The 100th Psalm. The Jesus prayer: "Lord Jesus Christ, Son of God, have mercy on me, a sinner." There's also one's own version of St. Patrick's Breastplate: "Christ be with me, Christ within me, Christ behind me, Christ before me, Christ beside me, Christ beneath me, Christ above me."

Even if all we can manage is a spontaneous, childlike cry from the heart, we need at such a time to call on God. God won't mind our fear, our despair, our self-pity, our anger. God is saddened only when we do not pray at all. Have no doubt that when we do pray, God hears and will console when we are ready for consolation.

Because eventually, after every crisis, there comes a time when we can breathe again and know that God wishes us well. There comes a time when we know we have done what we can to make reparation, when we are forgiven by God, when we can forgive ourselves. That's when we pick up and go on with our lives. We don't get over it when the worst happens. We go on in spite of it. That's how it has always been and always will be.

Thank You God for Your saving presence.

Seventy-seven

Barefoot Saturday Morning

October 2003

When the Lord saw that he had turned aside to see, God called to him out of the bush, "Moses, Moses!" And he said, "Here I am." Then he said, "Come no closer! Remove the sandals from your feet, for the place on which you are standing is holy ground."
— *Exodus 3:4,5*

In the quiet old Ravenna neighborhood of Seattle, the many trees are still fully leaved even though it's the middle of September. Skies are sunny and cloudy, and the air is fragrant.

Inside the house it's a barefoot Saturday morning for the five of us. Son-in-law Steve sits in the green easy chair reading a magazine, one bare foot on the floor and the other propped over a knee. His son Cody, age 8, twines his bare feet around the legs of a wooden chair as he plays a computer game. My daughter Sarah, new mom, sits by me on the burgundy sofa, her bare feet crossed in the graceful posture that seems to come to her naturally. She is reading a book of essays written by other new moms. I'm stretched out with my bare feet against the cushion between us. On my lap dozes grandson Adam, aged 2 ½ weeks. His miniscule bare feet are nearly sole to sole as they peek out from under the blue, bunny-covered receiving blanket.

Precious, contented, trusting, loving life; a couple of hours carved out and set aside from the usual commuting-working-schoolgoing-soccerplaying-baby-tending-housecleaning-shopping-cooking-laundrydoing-chorecompleting-appointmentkeeping-socializing daily routine of a growing American family. It's a time to recall God's presence among us, God's blessings upon us. It's a breathing space before four of us once again put on our shoes and hit the ground running.

Holy ground is found not only in the Bible, but wherever God's presence is recognized. In many religious traditions, shoes are removed in places set aside for worship. That way we are reminded not to carry into God's place the soil of commerce that clings to our shoes. We are also reminded of our infant-like powerlessness before God, and of our vulnerability to one another and to the chances and troubles of our lives.

Our living rooms of love and care are holy ground as well. For the Lord is present and where God is, is holy.

My prayer today is that you and yours also may spend many quiet, mindful, barefoot hours together.

Strengthen me God to appreciate the barefoot moments of my life.

Matthew Richard Conklin
1971 – 2003
November 2003

On October 13, our sweet, funny, kind, smart, sad and lost son Matthew died by his own hand. Your understanding, your gifts of food and flowers, your presence, your words and wordless hugs, your thoughts and prayers, are like firefly lights flickering softly through the dense black thicket of our grief. They remind us that, with God's help and yours, we will surely one day step again into the light.

Thank You God for Matthew.

Caroline and Bill Conklin

Seventy-eight

Shining Faces

December 2003

The Lord bless you and keep you;
the Lord make his face to shine upon you, and be
*   gracious to you;*
the Lord lift up his countenance upon you, and give
*   you peace. — Numbers 6:24-26.*

A story is told of one Brother Michael, who claimed to talk to God every week. A certain old brother monk was skeptical, and decided to expose Michael as a fraud. He said, "This week, Michael, when you talk to God, ask Him to tell you something only God and I know of. Ask him about the terrible thing I did when I was young."

The next week the skeptic went up to Michael. "Well, did you talk to God?"

"Oh yes."

"Did you ask him about my sin?"

Michael smiled at him. "I did."

"And?"

Michael smiled even more broadly. "God said He forgot."

The story came to my mind this week, when two things happened: First we received a photo of our 2½-month-old grandson Adam beaming up at his mother Sarah as she held him close in her arms. Then I read an essay in this month's "The Christian Century" by Miroslav Volf, a Yale Divinity School professor. He writes of the blessing phrase, "the Lord make his face shine upon you," comparing that image to the shining face of his own little son, gazing into his daddy's eyes.

I understood what he meant when I looked again at the photo of Adam and Sarah. The child was indeed regarding his mother with complete and utter approval

Yet how can the in-the-moment smiles of infants be compared to God's favor? Perhaps they can in this way: Like God, neither Volf's son nor our Adam dwells on past hurts or anticipates future ones. These little ones blame us for nothing, forgive us everything. They may help us to an understanding of how God's all-encompassing love and forgiveness is possible.

Still we wonder, how could God possibly shine wholeheartedly upon you and me, who have often wandered far from the Way? After all, God knows everything about us, and the dreadful things we're capable of doing. How can God possibly rejoice in us?

Volf writes, "God's shining face concerns our very being. It stands for God's sheer delight that we exist and live before him."

Some people see a condemning, judging God, always hard to please. I don't. I couldn't worship such a God, I'm afraid, and continue hopefully with

my life. The God I lean on loves, smile, forgives—
and forgets.

*Strengthen me God to accept Your forgiveness and
to go bravely on.*

Seventy-nine

Good News

January 2004

Then Jesus went about all the cities and villages, teaching in their synagogues, and proclaiming the good news of the kingdom, and curing every disease and every sickness. – Matthew 9:35

"Mom, I have news," Sarah said over the phone, three years ago.

"Oh?" I said, wary. Many of the messages we'd received from and about our children over the years have not been messages we wanted to receive. All three have struggled with relationships, jobs, depression, health, and just plain bad luck. I braced myself for another crisis and prayed I'd respond in the best way.

Sarah laughed at my tone. "Mom, not all news is bad!"

Then she told me that she and Steve, a fine man we had grown to care for and respect, were marrying. I was thrilled.

Afterwards, I thought about what she'd said, *Not all news is bad*. I do tend to expect the worst, and I don't think I'm the only one. Perhaps that's why Christianity emphasizes the Good News of Jesus Christ, because good news is rare in the human condition—rare, and precious. It is also what keeps us going in an often disappointing and terrifying world.

A year ago Sarah again called, saying, "Mom, I have news." Again my response was hesitant.

"Mom!" she said, laughing. "Not all news is bad, remember?"

She told me she was to have a baby in September. Of course I was delighted. Then, on September 1st, Steve called with the best news of all: that grandchild Adam Thomas Frey was born and thriving, and that Sarah was doing well. Not long after that, Sarah phoned with a request to have him baptized at Incarnation over their holiday visit. More good news!

Some of you were in church this December 28th and supported our family for that moving ceremony of Christian initiation. For me, it was a kind of sacred blending of the universal Good News of Jesus and our own family's personal good news of birth and continuance. Coming as it did after a year of terrible loss, the baptism was a true blessing. The memory of that Sunday morning at the font will linger in our minds and hearts. It will bring us hope for the future, and courage to face whatever happens.

You too may be struggling with a bleak midwinter. But God is merciful, and not all news is bad! May the coming year bring good news, and a deeper under-standing of the Good News of Jesus, to us all.

Thank You God for the good news in my life.

Eighty

Life in the Middle Distance
February 2004

Your word is a lamp to my feet and a light to my path.
— Psalm 119:105

We have lived in this Mountain View split-level for thirty years now. My favorite easy chair faces west. From there, I look out through the glass deck door across a field owned by the Roman Catholic Diocese to the tops of the trees at Mount Olive Cemetery. From dusk until dawn, a single light shines from among those trees. I expect it's a security light. But to me that light represents the light at the end of life, the light of God's promise, the light that shines for loved ones gone before.

My chair has its own lamp. In the early mornings I sit under its soft glow and pray, read, write, meditate. Sometimes I sit there too long, unmoving and unmotivated, gazing at the distant light. When a loved one dies, as our son Matthew did four months ago, it's easy to surrender to a sense of futility. *Why bother? Why try? Soon enough, that far-off light will be my light too. Maybe it's best just to wait quietly for my time to come.*

But recently Matthew's sister Mary came to visit. She brought to Bill and me her youth and energy, her plans and concerns, her enthusiasms.

She also brought a present. It's a flat black bowl holding three thick candles, colored cream, caramel and cranberry. Now every morning the lights from those three candles shine from our dining table between the distant light and the near one. They are in my "middle distance," an artist's term of perspective that means "between the foreground and the horizon."

Isn't that where life happens, really? Between right now and someday?

Contemplating those candles, I came to understand that while heaven is a promised hope and the present moment a fleeting gift, the *middle distance* is where life is planned and plans unfold. The middle distance is today's notes on the daily planner that we read each morning or that we keep in our heads. It is the how, why, when, where and who of our lives. It's the reason we put one foot in front of the other. God's word is a lantern to our feet, and those feet are not standing still but moving along an earthly path hour by hour.

We breathe within the moment, moving toward the middle distance, anticipating the faraway light of heaven.

Strengthen me God to live in the moment as I plan for the middle distances of my life.

Eighty-one

Breakthrough

March 2004

Blessed are the pure in heart, for they will see God.
— Matthew 5:8

My mother Blanche Roberts was especially close
to our oldest child Sarah. Mother loved all four of
our children, but with our first-born Sarah she had a
special bond.

When Sarah was ten, she flew alone, in the care
of the flight attendants, to Sonoma, California, where
she spent two weeks with my parents. Sarah remembers how good Mother was to her, how indulgent,
how accepting. She remembers her grandmother's
brilliant smile, and her laugh.

We all remember that smile, all her family and
friends, including some of you. (I know, because
you've told me.) Mother's smile involved her entire
face, and her laugh was whole-bodied. When Mother
smiled and when she laughed, she lightened the
burden for everyone around her for that moment.
Everyone felt a little better about something!

She lived to be one hundred years old, but she
was ageless when she laughed.

Less than a year after Mother died, Sarah gave
birth to baby Adam. Our one regret was that Mother

never met him. "But I think she sees him from where she is," we reassured each other.

In late January 2004, I visited Sarah and her family in Seattle. It was a magical time. Most mornings I went to where Sarah nursed Adam, and sat quietly near them. Five-month-old Adam always turned his head to gaze solemnly at me, an intruder on the sacred mother-child dyad. I smiled murmured, "Hi, Adam," and held my breath, waiting for what I hoped would come. It always did. After a moment his whole face—eyes and mouth, cheeks and chin— broke into a luminous smile and he gave a low full-bodied laugh. Of course Sarah and I smiled and laughed, too. It would be impossible not to.

Then one morning, as we all three shared joy, I seemed to hear a fourth laugh as well and to see another smile. Mother's? Of course, Mother's! Her dear wrinkled face and the child's smooth clear one seemed to blend for an instant and become the same. *She's here*, I thought. My heart leapt up. *She's well and she's here. Thank you, God.*

We are sometimes granted glimpses through the veil that separates this world from the one beyond. To recognize such a glimpse we need only keep our minds and hearts open to one another, and to God.

Thank You God for glimpses of heaven.

Eighty-two

Welcome Feet

April 2004

*Then he poured water into a basin and began to wash
the disciples' feet and to wipe them with a towel that
was tied around him. – John 13:5*

The nails of my misshapen toes are polished scarlet
and my normally rough heels are smooth. *Too much
information*, you say? Usually I would agree. But not
today. Today I am thinking about Maundy Thursday,
and the foot-washing we will do at the service of Holy
Eucharist before the Stripping of the Altar and the all-
night Vigil. It is arguably the most dramatic night of
our liturgical year, and the most humbling.

Last week in Seattle, daughter Sarah asked for a
pedicure for her birthday. As the mother of a seven-
month-old baby, she seldom has time for self-care.

"Will you have one, too?" she said.

"Oh no," I said. "My feet are too ugly. I hate my feet.
The pedicurist probably wouldn't even touch them."
Then I thought again. "But my feet have been good to
me really. They've taken me many many places."

"That's right, Mom," she said. "You should honor
your feet."

And so Sarah and I spent a sweet hour in a tiny
shop called Welcome Nails, as two Korean sisters,
sitting on low stools, efficiently ministered to us.

Of course I thought of Maundy Thursday, and how Jesus washed the disciples' feet before the Last Supper. The washing was needed. People in those days bathed before going to a dinner, but their feet got dusty as they walked from their house to the house where the dinner was being served. So their feet would be washed by servants before they entered. The feet of people who walked so much in sandals would not only be dirty, they would be cut, scarred, calloused, and sometimes misshapen as well. Peter objected because Jesus wanted to perform this menial, unlovely service for him. But Jesus insisted, speaking obliquely of baptism and of his death and resurrection soon to come.

At the April 8 Holy Eucharist, some of us will wash one another's feet. We will be doing what Jesus did. We will be ministering for Jesus, and to Jesus. Just as we will wait with Jesus at the garden Vigil as an act of devotion, so we will wash His feet as an act of service.

We who can walk, walk now for Jesus. We walk to do Jesus' work in the world. Our feet may never be beautiful by the world's standards but they are beautiful in their godly work for the very young, the very old, the poor, the ill, the sorrowful, the troubled, the defenseless, the dying.

It is good, on Maundy Thursday, to honor our own feet, and the feet of Jesus, and the feet of our church community, in gratitude and in humility.

Thank You God for my feet and for the places they have carried me in love.

Eighty-three

Holy Silence

May 2004

But the Lord is in his holy temple; let all the earth keep silence before him! – Habbukuk 2:20

Clergy Conference this year was at Camp Marshall, the Diocesan church property on Flathead Lake. It is a beautiful, beautiful place that every Montana Episcopalian should visit and re-visit .

For me, going there was bittersweet. I loved meeting again dear clergy friends whom I had not seen since our son Matthew died in October. All of them, even those who had heavy burdens of their own, gave me words and hugs of comfort. But I felt sad as well, because we used to go there with Matthew— first taking him as a Middler, and recently spending Family Week there with him and his wife and sons.

On Wednesday we met in Brewer Lodge to hear our speaker Sister Barbara Jean Brown, a witty little Episcopalian nun, talk to us about the prayerful life. She had many good things to tell us, but the best part was when she said nothing—and we said nothing. That was when Sister B.J. sent us off in Holy Silence. No talking at all.

Such silence is unusual for us Americans. We tend to fill all quiet hours with music or TV or telephone calls, or our own whirling, worldly thoughts. Holy Silence is meditative, contemplative. It's time spent quieting the noise from within, listening for God's still small voice, and letting nature's sounds filter through. At camp, the sounds were lake birds, chattering squirrels, lapping water, distant traffic, the crunch of feet, through the ground cover.

Mine was a slow-walking meditation, in which each step takes between five and ten seconds. My mind was on my steps, on Matthew, on God. First my feet took me slowly slowly down to the dock, through the chilly breeze into the warming sun. Then up and across, approaching the cabin by the shore where our son and his family stayed four years ago. But I didn't arrive there. As the Camp bell signaled the end of the hour, I turned and slowly made my way back. The walk gave me a peaceful, calming sense of God's time, the time in which Matthew now exists, the time which awaits us all.

Others used their hour differently. They sat very still gazing out over the lake, or they remained mindful of their breathing, or they repeated a simple prayer over and over. Each of us reported feeling better for the time set aside.

We don't need to be at Camp Marshall to take some Holy Silence. We surely can find time to give a few moments of our busy, noise-filled day over to God, starting with ten or twenty minutes or half an hour. A peaceful mind is our reward.

Strengthen me God to take long moments of Holy Silence.

Eighty-four

Summer Solstice
June 2004

When Elizabeth heard Mary's greeting, the child leaped in her womb. And Elizabeth was filled with the Holy Spirit and exclaimed with a loud cry, "Blessed are you among women, and blessed is the fruit of your womb." – Luke 1:41, 42

June 24, which happens to be the 13th anniversary of my ordination to the diaconate, is the Feast of the Nativity of St. John the Baptist. It is exactly six months from Christmas Eve, when John's younger cousin Jesus was born. When Mary visited her relative Elizabeth early in Mary's pregnancy, the child that leaped in Elizabeth's womb was John.

June 24 and December 24 coincide very closely with the Summer Solstice, when the hours of sunlight are longest and begin to decrease, and the Winter Solstice, when the hours of sunlight are shortest and begin to increase. Many Christian holidays were made to coincide with pagan ones, in order that the new religion might gain acceptance. Long ago, June 24 was known as the Summer Christmas and was celebrated with feasting, dancing, music, bonfires and the giving of gifts.

Even longer ago, from the dawn of human time, the people celebrated the long day of Summer Solstice as they thanked the sun for warmth, light, color and all growing things, and begged the sun never to abandon them forever. Then, six months later, they rejoiced at the sun's slow and steady return.

Nowadays Summer Solstice is celebrated by groups of people all over the world, as they gather in places that inspire awe—a mountain top or a riverside at sunrise. They feast, they dance and chant, they rejoice in the beauty and the abundance of life.

For Christians, however, the juxtaposition of John and the Solstice seem incongruous. It's hard to reconcile the angry, ascetic, locust-eating John even with his own Feast Day, let alone with the open enjoyment of the earth and its bounty that is found at Summer Solstice. It may help to remember that we are not celebrating John's adulthood, when human sin had grieved him so much that he felt moved to renounce all comforts. We are celebrating the tiny John who leaped for joy in his mother's womb, the plump and healthy baby John, laughing with his smaller cousin Jesus in so many Italian Renaissance paintings. All thriving babies love life and its pleasures. All new humans love the sights, sounds, tastes, smells, feel of the world and the people around them.

Jesus makes all things new. That includes you and me. Perhaps June 24 is the perfect time for us to step away from our adult burdens and resentments, and recognize that the earliest joys of our lives can also be our present joys. Maybe it's a good time to get out of our rooms and our routines and stand on a hill or by water with our hands raised to God and God's beautiful, sunlit world. To give thanks for the seasons and their primal, heartfelt pleasures. To celebrate God in body as well as in spirit with feasting, dancing, music, bonfires, and the giving of gifts.

Thank You God for Your holy days of summer, and the bounty that they bring.

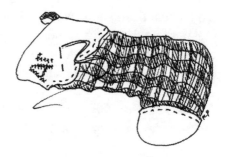

Eighty-five

Christmas Stockings in the Summertime
August 2004

Let the favor of the Lord our God be upon us,
and prosper for us the work of our hands—
O prosper the work of our hands! - Psalm 90:17

The stocking that develops tiny square by tiny square between my fingers will depict a man and a boy with a dog dragging a cut evergreen tree past a live tree, a snowman and a red barn. Their destination is a yellow farmhouse with smoke rising from the chimney. It's the fifth of the seven grandchild-stockings I'll make. They've been done one by one as each child entered the family: first Mary's girl and boy, then Matthew's step-son and older boy, and now Sarah's step-son; next Matthew's youngest and then Sarah's baby.

My cross stitchery usually has to be lined, because the back isn't so neat as it should be. Oh well. We do the best we can. Besides, the grandchild won't care about that, nor about my getting somewhat confused in the many colors of the large tree in the front of the picture. It still looks pretty! Besides that, every stitch contains kind thoughts for the recipient.

That's probably the best thing about stitchery projects. As we sew, we think about the person for whom the object is intended. We send good wishes their way. Some other advantages of hand-stitching as a hobby are these: It is a social activity because one faces the room, and can talk and sew at the same time. It can be done while care-taking, since it may be left off and picked up quickly. It engages both sides of the brain, and so helps keep one sharp. It relaxes.

Christmas and other holy day stitchery may also turn the mind to thoughts of Christ's incarnation, life, death and resurrection. It may remind us of our own past Christmases, with joyous memories and bitter-sweet ones. Last year we had four retired stocking labels on our tree: those of my parents and those of our two sons. By the grace of God, no other stockings will need to be retired this year. But that is out of our hands.

Out of our hands. What's in our hands is our work of the day, whatever it may be.

By the end of the week, I hope to have stitched the snow at the toe, heel and sole of this stocking.

Then I can work upwards through the barn, house, mountain and sky, and finally can stitch the name: **Cody**. *Be well, young Cody,* say my heart, mind and fingers. *Be safe, be happy, and be well.*

Thank You God for the work of my hands.

Eighty-six

The Patio Door

September 2004

Look mercifully upon this man and this woman who come to you seeking your blessing, and assist them with your grace... – The Book of Common Prayer, p. 425

The September 2004 <u>Guideposts</u> magazine carries a story I wrote about Bill's and my early marriage. It's called "Piece of Cake." My pre-nuptial counselees may recognize the story, because I've often told it to illustrate the importance to a marriage of humor and compromise.

Long story short: One dinner time, while Bill was still in law school, I was scolding him about something minor when he reached across the table with a butter knife and sliced my piece of cake in two. After a shocked pause, I began to laugh and so did he. And so a problem that might have escalated resolved itself.

In a long-term marriage, such stories stay fresh because the couple refers to them again and again.

Another shared memory we have is of a long ago <u>New Yorker</u> cartoon. It showed a bedroom with peeling plaster and one bare light bulb hanging from the ceiling. In the bed is a slovenly woman with her hair every which way and a slip strap dragging down one arm. Through the door comes her equally slovenly husband wearing an undershirt, cigarette dangling from his mouth. In his hand is a steaming cup of coffee, meant for her.

She says to him in the caption something like this, *"Louie, you're a regular jewel!"*

Why did that cartoon appeal to us so strongly that we would say that line to one another many times over the years? Because it seems to say that caring and graciousness are inward treasures, unrelated to one's age, beauty, or situation in life.

I'm thinking of that cartoon today because of our patio's sliding door. Gradually it had become more and more difficult to use. I couldn't open it without using both hands and bracing myself. To close it, I had to get behind and shove. Then it slammed in with such force as to endanger our small pets. (I expect they learned to be wary.)

Today Bill took the door off and put it back with replacement rollers that work smoothly.

"Louie," I said, as I gleefully and easily slid the door back and forth, "you're a regular jewel!"

Bill smiled.

By now, for us, such memories become bitter-sweet as the years of the past number so many more than the years of the future possibly can. Neither Bill nor I is sick, so far as we know, but the time we have left together is limited at best, and may be very short indeed. The recent sudden death of our son has made that starkly clear. Such unlooked-for losses remind us that *Thanks for everything* can never be said too soon, or too often.

Thank You God for gratitude expressed.

Eighty-seven

Second Thought

November 2004

If I speak in the tongues of mortals and of angels, but do not have love, I am a noisy gong or a clanging cymbal. - 1 Corinthians 13:1

For several years, I studied Spanish. Once a week I drove across town to Skyline School for a two-hour class in Spanish Conversation with an exuberant native of Columbia named Nancy. Last year I finally gave myself permission to quit. I can, and do, read Spanish. I can even converse with a patient, Spanish-speaking person. But I will never be fluent. What I came to realize is that Spanish will, for me, always be a "second thought." I must always translate for myself. First English. Then Spanish. Actually I realized that some time ago. What's recent is my reconciling myself to my non-fluency, and deciding it's okay.

The selfless language of God is, for most of us, also a second thought, also a translation. But it's okay. Few can speak with perfect fluency the language of the Other Person, whether the person is a South African or your own neighbor or even your parent, spouse, child. Self-interest comes first and is not easily by-passed. It takes conscious effort. If speaking in the tongue of the Other Person came easy, God wouldn't have had to send Jesus to interpret.

Take a baby in a crib, crying because she is hungry, wet, cold or sick. She is terrifyingly vulnerable, and her needs must come first to her. She can't be generous, take her parents' late-night party into consideration and let them sleep. If she's quiet, she may die. When she cries, help comes. Her selfishness is necessary for her survival.

It's true that some people are so deprived or neglected or abused as children that they can never get beyond the primal fear for their own survival. (It's this fear, I've come to believe, that underlies much of our anger and hatred.) But most of us have had our basic needs met and can, by God's grace and by making an effort, step into another person's shoes long enough to accept them as fully human like ourselves, and to do what we can to help them.

After seeing a documentary about AIDs orphans in Uganda, Jake said to his pastor, "I must be a terrible person. When I saw those suffering children my first thought was, 'Thank God my kids and grandkids aren't like that!"

"And your second thought?" the pastor said. Jake said, "The documentary gave the address of a helping agency. I mailed a check." The pastor said, "That's all God asks. God doesn't fault you for the first thought that runs through your mind. It's what you think and do next that matters."

All the world's religions ask Compassion of their followers; all recognize that achieving it isn't easy. If we can study Compassion as a second and difficult language, our words will not be as sounding brass or tinkling symbols. We will understand one another, help one another, and God will rejoice.

Strengthen me God to learn and to speak the language of compassion.

Eighty-eight

Dear Santa

December 2004

Give us grateful hearts, our Father, for all your mercies, and make us mindful of the needs of others; through Jesus Christ our Lord. **Amen** – *The Book of Common Prayer, p. 835*

Dear Santa,

It's Caroline. I know you haven't heard from me in, well, decades. The last time I wrote I was living in Cleveland with my parents and sisters, and my last name was Roberts. But we have a chimney in this house, too.

I've been very good this year. So here goes. I don't wear much jewelry, but I do like rings with colored gemstones. I have red, blue, green and milky white. So I think purple would be nice this year. You can get me a pretty amethyst ring in a gold setting for not much more than $200. If you wouldn't mind. That's all. Thanks a lot.

<u>Santa:</u> Define "very good."

<u>Me:</u> Beg pardon?

<u>Santa</u>: Forget it. Instead, think again about that $200 plus dollars. Do you know what else that money would buy besides another shiny ring?

<u>Me</u>: Well I…let's see … four months of cable TV? A party dress? A few meals with wine at Tony Roma's?

<u>Santa</u>: You aren't trying. I'll go first: Two hundred dollars will buy one hundred and twelve meals for down-and-out people at the Great Falls Rescue Mission.

<u>Me</u>: Oh. (sigh) Okay. Hmm. Two hundred dollars would pay for 16 months tuition for an impoverished child at a school in Central America through Food for the Poor. Or a sewing machine through the same organization, so a single mom or dad can start a business. In some parts of the world, $200 would go a long way toward funding a Habitat for Humanity house.

<u>Santa</u>: That's the idea.

<u>Me</u>: From America's Second Harvest, $200 will buy nearly 800 bags of food for hungry families. From the Heifer Project, $240 will buy two goats or two sheep or two pigs to help a family become self-sustaining.

<u>Santa</u>: I thought those organizations would appeal to you. In Cleveland, when you were eight, you asked me for a Cut-and- Paste Farm Kit. And got it, by the way.

<u>Me:</u> But how do I know if a charity is any good? The administrators may be taking a big cut for themselves.

<u>Santa:</u> Look on the internet. Several Charity Watch organizations have researched this for you. Anyway, the ones you've mentioned are all good.

<u>Me:</u> But I can't see any of those things, Santa. I can't pass them down to my girls.

<u>Santa:</u> I thought you were supposed to have an imagination. You can't see in your mind's eye a smiling Third World child learning life skills? A formerly disheartened, angry man finally able to put food on his family's table? You can't pass down to your girls a world that's a little better because of what you've done?

<u>Me:</u> You made your point. Forget the ring. I'll get back to you.

<u>Santa</u>: I thought you would. Catch you later.

<u>Me:</u> (after a pause) Are you sure you're Santa Claus?

But there was no reply.

Thank You God for charity organizations that allow us to help others.

Eighty-nine

Checking the Baggage

January 2005

'Tis the gift to be simple, 'tis the gift to be free…- Hymn
"Simple Gifts," words by Shaker Elder Joseph Brackett Jr.

Many years ago, Bill bought me a big, soft-sided maroon suitcase at Kaufman's. When I'm traveling for longer than a weekend, I pull it from the closet, lift it onto the bed and pack it. Once it's zipped and ready to go, I lug it down the stairs, into the garage and the car, and haul it out again at the airport. At the airline counter I show my ID, hoist the suitcase onto the scale, and watch as it is placed on the moving belt and disappears. Walking away from the ticket counter with only my boarding pass and my carry-on purse, I feel a real sense of freedom and lightness. For a time, anyway, my heavy baggage is out of my hands.

This year, as we walk away from the Old Year into the New, I've decided to try to retain that sense of freedom and lightness. Instead of making resolutions, I'll pack up some useless internal baggage and send it off. If I can do that, a couple of long-time, unresolved resolutions might just take care of themselves.

So I haul out a big, soft-sided, sky-blue imaginary suitcase, lay it on the bed, open it, and start packing.

First I'll put in a couple of major Resentments and Grudges, bulky things that I've been carrying around for some time now. They've done me no good; they've done no one any good, and it's time to send them away.

On top of those I'll lay a dozen assorted Regrets, and try to eliminate *if only, I should have*, and *how could I* from my internal vocabulary. Learning from mistakes needn't mean re-living them over and over.

Into the corners of the suitcase I'll stick several Envies, of people who seem to be better off than I in one way or another. All lives have space for joy and trouble both.

Next I'll fill in those uneven places with some Baseless Worries. They're scratchy and uncomfortable, and never did fit any real situation.

That's a lot of stuff, but this suitcase seems to be infinitely spacious. Might as well throw in several of those painful Embarrassing Moments. Most of them happened a long time ago and have been forgotten by everybody else. Even if they happened yesterday, what's done is done.

I zip the suitcase, close my eyes, and send it off with a prayer. When I open my eyes again the suitcase is gone. With luck, I'll never see it again.

Strengthen me God to set aside permanently the unneeded mental baggage of my life.

Ninety

Hearts in the Right Place

February 2005

Light dawns for the righteous, and joy for the upright in heart. – Psalm 97:11

My parents wouldn't take me to see "The Wizard of Oz" the first time it came to the movie theater near our Cleveland, Ohio, home. Probably they'd been warned by friends that the green-faced witch could give a small child nightmares. (Which she certainly could, did, and continues to do.)

Of course I saw it the next time around, and have seen it countless times since. Like many other people, I can recite large chunks of script. But there's one line that I never have quite understood.

The story, as a reminder:

Dorothy, the Scarecrow, the Cowardly Lion and the Tin Man are promised by the Wizard that if they kill the Wicked Witch they will receive, respectively, a trip home, brains, courage, and a heart. They do, and the phony but generous Wizard tries to give them what they need.

To the Tin Man he gives a clunky necklace with a clock set in a plump, shiny red heart. He says, "Remember, my sentimental friend, that a heart is judged not by how much you love, but by how much you are loved by others."

What does that mean, exactly? That unloving people aren't loved, I suppose. It's expanding on the original line from the L. Frank Baum book. There the Wizard cuts open the Tin Man's chest and inserts a small red-silk, sawdust-filled heart, making sure to put it "in the right place." Having your heart in the right place, I think, means trying to do the selfless thing, even if not always succeeding. It means letting one's heart "go out" to others. One who does that will be loved.

Be that as it may, both book and movie make clear that no one received anything they didn't already have. They just didn't know they had it!

Certainly all their hearts were in the right place. When Toto the dog pulls open the curtain and exposes the phony Wizard manipulating his flashy machinery, the friends are at first angry, then anxious. If the Wizard has no real power, how can they receive what they've endured so much to earn? Yet each asks not for their own gift but gifts for the others. *What about the Scarecrow? The Tin Man? What about the Lion? And Dorothy?*

Valentines Day comes this month. It's a good time to show ourselves that our hearts, too, are in the right place. How? One way is to begin Valentines Day, and every other day, by praying for each person we know who is in pain, trouble, isolation, or danger. Not only will these prayers help them, they will help us to keep our perspective and to take ourselves and our own desires less seriously.

Thank You God for stories that celebrate the good in us.

Ninety-one

Snow Days

March 2005

O God, in the course of this busy life, give us times of refreshment and peace; and grant that we may so use our leisure to rebuild our bodies and renew our minds, that our spirits may be opened to the goodness of your creation; through Jesus Christ our Lord. ***Amen***

- The Book of Common Prayer, p. 825

Now that I'm long out of school, and retired from an 8 to 4 day as a Speech Pathologist for the school system, I enjoy my Snow Days more than ever.

On a Snow Day, schools are closed because of the weather. When I was a child, and woke to white flakes floating past my bedroom window, I listened hard to the radio hoping for an announcement: *"The following schools are closed: Harrison. Washington. Hilltop..."* What joy if my school was one of them! Eventually, the rules tightened. By the time I was teaching, Snow Days had to be made up at the end of the year.

But I maintain that a true Snow Day never has to be made up. A true Snow Day is sent by the Weather Fairies and is extra. It is the 366th day in a non-Leap Year. It is a day when no aging occurs, and no weight is gained. Snow falls softly and steadily, whiting everything that is dark, rounding ragged outlines, muffling harsh sounds. Snow makes a Grandma's quilt of tranquility.

We may be out of Snow Days for the season. But there are still Rain Days, Heat Days, Fifth Saturdays, and Just Because Days. Over-conscientious working people may need to be creative and take an occasional Mental Health Day.

We all have long, relentless lists of duties for the various aspects of our lives. When one thing gets done something else pops up, like mechanical ducks in a shooting gallery. At night we fall into bed, our sleep troubled by the next day's duties. What do we do on a Snow Day? Whatever our inner selves long to do that our sense of duty won't allow on a regular day.

Here's some of what I did on my last Snow Day: read, wrote, watched an old movie on television, stitched on a grandchild's Christmas stocking, cooked and ate vegetable curry soup, napped, meditated with scented candles, listened to a Verdi opera. The next day I was refreshed and ready to get back to work.

You'll have your own wishes and ways for days like this. Maybe you'll want to drive somewhere or nowhere, play outside with the kids, build a model plane, watch a game or a match. The important thing is to commit to your Snow Day as you do to a duty day. God prescribed a periodic day of rest for the good of our souls. A Snow Day can be a Sabbath, of sorts, and we can thank God for it.

Thank You God for the Snow Days of my life.

Ninety-two

Making Time Good

April 2005

For everything there is a season, and a time for every matter under heaven. – Ecclesiastes 3:1

A woman drove quickly and skillfully down the highway as her husband dozed beside her. Smoothly she passed everything in sight. The hours went by. Her husband wakened, looked around, sat up straight. "Wait a minute!" he said. "We're supposed to be driving east, but the sun is setting in front of us!"

She sighed. "I know," she said. "But we're making such good time!"

We often "make good time" in the wrong direction, sometimes for years and years. Since we can't see into the future, we take the road that lies open whether or not that road is right for us. But meanwhile, many hours are our very own, and during those hours we can mindfully "make time good."

How can we do that? Jesus tells us. Time spent in prayer and meditation is "good time." Time used to help the poor and needy is "good time." So is time taken to bring joy, comfort, love, encouragement to ourselves or to someone else.

We realize this when we pass time with the very old or the very young.

For the very old, time has lost all urgency. A few years ago I sat with my mother as she lay dying in her Missoula bedroom. Time slowed to the pace of her breathing. When I left occasionally to do errands among all the busy people, their busyness seemed wrong. Why were they racing around like that? What was the hurry? Better to sit in a quiet room as the thin white curtains puffed inward with the breeze, as the light shifted around the blue vase of yellow roses on the night stand. I sat remembering past times, past places, when mother was the quick, sure one and I only followed along.

It was a great gift, although overwhelmingly sad, to be there for her last breath taken in this world, as she had been there for my first.

For the very young, on the other hand, every minute is exciting.

Just before Lent my daughter Sarah came to visit, bringing her 18-month-old son Adam. He sat on the playroom floor, absorbed in forming and re-forming wooden blocks. He seemed to be thinking: *If I push this, then this happens! Look at that! You build the tower, I knock it down! Now I build one, and you knock it down! Life is good.* I gazed at, laughed with and helped tend the child for virtually their whole visit, letting everything else slide except the daily chores. Wasted time? Oh dear no. Not wasted for us, because Adam taught us so much about living life fully. Not wasted for him, because he was gaining not only in knowledge of the world but in depth and breadth of family love

Anything that brings the sweetness of life to our minds is Good Time.

Strengthen me God to make good the times of my life.

Ninety-three

Under the White Cloth

May 2005

Jesus said to (Mary Magdalene) "Do not hold on to me, because I have not yet ascended to the Father..."
- *John 20:17a*

A newcomer, glancing into the sacristy on her way to the sanctuary from the parish hall, says: "Sometimes there's a lumpy white cloth on the counter. What's under there? Always the same things?"

Probably we say something like: "Oh, those are the things for the communion service—vessels, bread, water, wine. Soon they'll be on the altar. And yes, they're always the same."

It's true that the service of Holy Eucharist, Holy Communion, doesn't change, or changes only when a new Book of Common Prayer is introduced. But looked at another way, the service changes constantly. Why? Because God is a living God, and because we communicants are always changing.

If we felt inspired that day, we might say to the newcomer, "What's under the white cloth is refreshment and renewal. What's under there is hope."

Hope. Any single week can bring to any one of us the devastating death of hope. A doctor shakes her head over an x-ray. A boss pink-slips a young father struggling to meet expenses. A phone call announces a fatal accident in another state. A longed-for person writes *"The thing is, I never loved you."* Mary Magdalene enters a tomb, and the corpse she came to honor has disappeared. Over and over again, darkness shrouds a hope that seems gone forever.

But then comes the Easter of the Eucharist. The cloth comes off, the altar shines with new life. An operation eases suffering. A job opens at a more suitable place. An estranged family is reunited by an accident. An old friend phones, *"I've always loved you, didn't you know?"* We gain new hope as, in the Bible, a "gardener" by the empty tomb turns out to be Jesus, and Mary Magdalene gains new hope.

But just as our lives can't return to exactly how they were before our troubles, Mary Magdalene's life couldn't return to how things were before the crucifixion. When an old hope dies it is gone, and the new hope is something we must grow into. Realizing the gardener was Jesus, Mary Magdalene tried to touch him. "Don't hold on to me," he said. He wasn't being unkind. He knew that change had come not only to him, who would soon ascend to God, but to her. Without his presence she would grieve, would grow, would adjust to the different way things were. He might have said, *You can't hold on to me. There's no need because I will hold on to you.* He didn't. That was something Mary would have to discover for herself.

The centuries-old objects, words and gestures of Holy Communion remind us that God stays the same yesterday, today, and tomorrow. We cannot predict what any week will bring, or the form our new hopes will take, or how they will change and shape us. We cannot confidently keep our grasp on God. But we can be confident that God's grip on us is strong and sure.

"What's under that cloth? Hope renewed. Always the same? No, never."

Thank You God for the holy communions of my life.

Ninety-four

God Be With You!

June 2005

The Lord will keep your going out and your coming in from this time on and forevermore. – Psalm 121:8

Summertime isn't all picnics, baseball and hiking trips. Often summertime means parting. It's now that our young people make their life-altering decisions. They go off to college, or to a job somewhere else, or they marry and re-locate. Summer means youth on the move, and youth on the move means teens and twenty-somethings saying goodbye. One moment they're noisily there, needing our attention. The next moment, they are gone. The quiet can be deafening. Part of us wants to keep our children and grand-children, our nieces and nephews, our godsons and daughters, near to us always. But we can't do that. We wouldn't if we could. We know that God's plan for their lives must unfold.

It's okay to feel sadness at parting, but we can save those tears for later on. Instead, we send them off cheerfully, with three special gifts:

1) Our belief in their abilities and their choices.

Do you remember the adults who reassured you, when you were young, that you were capable and ready for what was coming next? I do, and what they said meant a lot—even more than I quite realized at the time. Our young people are worried too, even though they may not show it. Picture their shiny new lives in your mind. See them in those lives, thriving. Tell them what you see.

2) A personal reminder that we care for them.

Often I give graduates a specially-chosen book from my collection. It may be a little worn and marked up, but that's okay. When I left my job in New York to get married, a co-worker gave me her favorite large kitchen spoon. When I use that spoon I think of her, and of those long-ago days, and smile. Any gift that contains the giver is enhanced.

3) Our faith in a loving God.

Our belief that God works for good in our lives and is always there to help and empower can be the best gift of all. "Goodbye" is short for "God be with you." Sometimes I like to say it just that way. I also like to pass on these words:

The Lord is your keeper;
The Lord is your shade at your right hand.
The sun shall not strike you by day, nor the moon
    by night.
The Lord will keep you from all evil;
he will keep your life.
The Lord will keep your going out and your
    coming in
from this time on, and forevermore.- *Psalm 121:5-8*

Thank You God for loved ones starting soon on a new journey.

Ninety-five

Thankful Daddy

July 2005

Oh Lord my God, I will give thanks to you forever.
- Psalm 30:12b

Our daughter Sarah, our son-in-law Steve and their two boys Cody and Adam have a family ritual. Before the evening meal, everyone holds hands around the table and names one thing they are thankful for that day.

When I visited in May, 20-month-old Adam could hardly wait for us all to sit down. When we did he beamed, spreading wide his small arms so we could take hands. Then, solemnly, he said, "Thankful Daddy."

Sarah translated. "That means, 'I'm thankful today for Daddy.'"

Then Adam looked at each of us in turn, and kept looking until we named something. Anything. It could be "I'm thankful today that I passed the test." Or that the test was cancelled. Or that my work project is finally moving along. Or "I'm thankful today for the blue bird in the back yard." Or for the good book from the library. Or for the delicious-smelling pasta dish on the table. Or for something grand like Life or Health or Family. Each offering is accepted and appreciated all around.

That done, Adam nodded, released hands, and we were free to eat—which we did with grateful, cheerful hearts.

We all need times of giving thanks. The habit of regular and specific gratitude brings to the front of our minds the many gifts we have been given, while at the same time allowing our fears and disappointments fade into the background.

Gratitude is not only cheering, it is empowering. Why? Because thankfulness leads to that other great virtue: *Hope*. Hope for the best comes when we recall the good that was, and is, and will be. It is hope that keeps us up and moving, while hope's dark opposite, cynicism, permits us to do nothing but sit around and despair.

Hope is the only real road to change. It is grateful, hopeful people who build the houses in Haiti, fight meth addiction in Great Falls, help preserve the environment and work to overcome poverty and feed the hungry everywhere. Grateful, hopeful people raise grateful, hopeful children, who will carry on when they are gone.

Young Adam doesn't exactly understand all this. But deep down he seems to know that to have family and friends touching as they speak gratitude from their hearts is a very, very good thing indeed.

Thank You God for Your many gifts to me.

Ninety-six

Misplaced at Birth

August 2005

And Jesus said to (the scribe), "Foxes have holes, and birds of the air have nests, but the Son of Man has nowhere to lay his head."- Matthew 8:20

My birthday is coming up. One year I received this card from daughter Sarah. It showed a woman of a certain age and read:

Of Royal Blood
Mysteriously Misplaced at Birth.
We're Honored to Celebrate your Regal Day
Happy Birthday, Highness

Misplaced people. Aliens. We think of aliens as people far from home who may look or speak or behave differently from the people who lived there first. Millions of people are displaced, are alien, and more every day, because of war, revolution, ethnic unrest, poverty, and environmental disaster.

In this country, one can be alien and displaced without ever leaving home. Think of the Native Americans, here first, yet almost immediately pushed into alien status. Think of the people in New Orleans and other coastal cities, alien long before they were forced from their homes by water. Virtually all poor, they had no fallback resources when trouble came, and no place to be when they were finally rescued. The whole experience only underscored what we seldom acknowledge: that the poor are indeed alien from mainstream American consumer society.

Right now the spotlight is on the plight of the poor. As the government once again cuts social programs, churches, mainline church people are protesting and may have a chance to be heard. A UN summit against poverty will be held, protesting the increasing concentration of wealth in the hands of a few.

We are Christians, followers of the Jesus who had much to say about economic injustice and the plight of the poor. God requires that we practice love toward outsiders and share what we have. As Christians, we are to exhort others to do the same.

Jesus lived as an alien, with no place to lay his head. All of us, if we go back far enough through our ancestors, can number aliens among them. Let's be proud of, and grateful for, our alien status. We know that all of God's children are of royal blood, mysteriously misplaced at birth—you and I, and the poorest of the poor anywhere on this earth. May we reflect this certain knowledge of our underlying kinship in our prayers, our actions and our words.

Strengthen me God to remember, when I react against distant others, that I'm an alien too.

Ninety-seven

Sophomores for God

September 2005

We are fools for the sake of Christ... - *1 Corinthians 4:10a*

It's back-to-school time for students, and back to Sunday school as well. I've been thinking lately about the Confirmation class I attended my sophomore year at Harvard/Radcliffe, and about being a Sophomore in general.

As class designations go, Sophomore is the only one that's puzzling. Freshmen are, well, fresh. Juniors have two years to go, and Seniors only one. But Sophomore is not so easily understood. Actually it comes from two Greek words meaning "wise fool." Not a bad description, when you think of it. The learning second-year students have acquired is mostly free-floating. They know their way around the campus but aren't sure yet which paths they want to follow. They have, hopefully, "beginner minds." ("In the beginner's mind there are many possibilities but in the expert's there are few." *Zen Master Suzuki-Roshi*). Sophomores are full of contradictions and potential.

I was far from home and lonely when I walked into the centuries-old, white painted Christ Church

Cambridge that slushy New England winter of my second year as a Radcliffe student. When I walked out again weeks later, I was still far from home but feeling less alone in the universe. The Rev. "Red" Kellogg was Student Chaplain. He met with our class weekly in his oak-paneled, book-filled office, and talked to us about some of the radical and contra-dictory beliefs of the Church. They struck a chord with me then. Now, many years later, I'm even more convinced that he was right.

Here is what he conveyed to me:

In a world of people obsessed by money and power, we believe that the poorest and most vulnerable of us are as valuable as are billionaires and government heads

In a world of people needing to take control, we believe that ultimately God is at the helm.

In a world of people bent on violence and revenge, we believe that only peace and forgiveness can set us free.

In a world of people driven by time-management, we believe that quiet hours of prayer and meditation are well-spent.

In a world of people convinced that science has all the answers, we believe that the most important truths will always be elusive and mysterious.

In many ways I'm a Sophomore still, and proud of it. I should like to have a beginner mind until the end of my days. I should like always to be open and searching, taking unanticipated paths and finding truths in unexpected places. You too? Then we'll be wise-fools for God together!

Thank You God for my moments of wise-foolishness.

Ninety-eight

May I See Clearly, Lord

October 2005

For now we see in a mirror, dimly, but then we will see face to face. - *1 Corinthians 13:12a*

Several years ago I began seeing poorly in low light, and night-driving became problematic. Last month, because print had begun to go hazy—much as though I were reading through rain—I underwent cataract surgery. The lenses replacing the cataracts are corrective, so that I went from being near-sighted to far-sighted in the space of a week. It's amazing, really. Without glasses or contacts, I can recognize you from way down the street. I can wake in the night and see the clock. I can read piano music on the rack, and see this computer screen, too. Now I need glasses only for reading.

How I would have loved this ability when I was a child, so embarrassed to be sent home for my glasses one day that I stayed there and had to be fetched. (I told my mother I'd been sent home because I was sick.) Or when in high school I tried to impress a date by leaving my glasses at home. (I impressed him all right, by bumping into things and missing the point of the blurry movie.) Or when, on a trip from Indiana to college in Boston in the 1950's, we unexpectedly had to change trains at Grand Central Station in New York City at 4 a.m., and I couldn't immediately lay hands on either my glasses or my contact lenses. With the help of God through a kindly stranger, I actually found the right train in time.

But that was then, and I got along fine. Just because this gift has come late in my life doesn't make it any less potentially valuable. I say "potentially," because all abilities can be used rightly or wrongly. We miss the point of any gift unless we seek God's guidance to use it well.

The Bible is filled with references to vision and sight, but usually not the eye-chart-reading kind. Even if our visual acuity more resembles the mole's than the eagle's, we all have an equal chance to see life truly, to see it God's way. Jesus had far better than 20-20 vision. He saw through the world's self-serving lies to find truth everywhere and in holy in everyone. By the grace of God, we can do that too.

Thank You God for all I see with Your gift of sight.

Ninety-nine

Contradictory November

November 2005

On this mountain the Lord of hosts will make for all
  peoples
a feast of rich food, a feast of well-aged wines,
of rich food filled with marrow, of well-aged wines
  strained clear.
And he will destroy on this mountain
the shroud that is cast over all peoples,
the sheet that is spread over all nations;
he will swallow up death forever. - Isaiah 25:6-7

November skies can be dull gray or bright blue. It's a month of contradiction. Beginning and ending in solemn contemplation of life's brevity, November swells in the middle with abundant feasting, as together we thank God for life's simple and infinitely precious pleasures. This reading from Isaiah, one that is often used at funerals, pretty much says it all.

We begin November with All Saints Day, and a listing of the recently departed members of our church community. I well remember how hard it was for me to hear that list a few short months after our little son Tom died in 1971; how I cried and kept on crying under gray November skies. The skies stayed gray, yet four weeks later Thanksgiving was here, and so were dear friends Jim and Anne, who had traveled to be with us for the holiday. And so we feasted together richly, and the shroud that had been cast over my heart was lifted. That Thanksgiving we truly captured the meaning of the holy-day, the weathering together of ills and trials.

Finally at the end of the month comes Advent, a penitential season. Now we move into quiet, blue-hued contemplation of the coming and brief sojourn on earth of our Lord Jesus Christ. The sojourn of our son Matthew, who died in 2003 at the age of 32, was brief as well. All our earthly sojourns seem brief, no matter how many years we accumulate, but some are painfully so.

I'm re-living my own losses because you and I need to understand that the grief of some of our church family members is as sharp and as raw and as cruel as ours once was. We need to be with these newly bereaved in any way that we can.

We who grieve know in our hearts that our loved ones would not want us to sit huddled in dark rooms, mourning. They would want us to celebrate their lives, to live fully our own, to cherish those who still walk the earth with us, to anticipate our eventual reunion. What we still have becomes all the more precious when we recall what we have lost. It's the contrast between light and shadow in November skies, and in our hearts, that gives depth and meaning to each day in this month, and in the months to come.

Strengthen me God to empathize with the grief of those around me.

One hundred

This Time, a Wedding

December 2005

Grant that their wills may be so knit together in your will, and their spirits in your Spirit, that they may grow in love and peace with you and one another all the days of their life. **Amen** – The Book of Common Prayer, p. 429

There have been too many funerals in our family these past few years. Happily, this time there was a wedding, a picture-perfect wedding in Boise's beautiful St. Michael's Episcopal Cathedral. The bride Cousin Nicole is a lawyer; the groom Nikolaus a West Point graduate recently returned from Iraq with a Bronze Star for heroism in combat. As they exchanged vows, we gathered "dearly beloved" felt our spirits rise with renewed hope for a future that has such young people in it.

In a pre-wedding counseling session years ago, a young woman asked me if the phrase "Until we are parted by death" could be omitted from the vows. I said that the words had less to do with eventual tragedy than with present commitment, and they stayed in.

She had a point, though. Marriage is not a single story ending in separation or the death of one of the parties any more than it is a single story of "happily ever after." Marriage is a long series of stories beginning with the proposal and wedding and continuing down through the years. It's not how a marriage—or a person—ends that matters. It's the manner of life along the way. Good-hearted, caring, industrious people bring hope to the world, and such people are found in any age and station of life. To me, the youth and promise of a young bride and groom symbolize the continuing potential for right action in all of us, working together, so long as we live on this earth.

Everyone at a wedding has stories to bring from it. I'll especially remember two from this one. First, I recall watching the wedding party and the congregation settle into misty-eyed contemplation as Cousin Pete's skillful, heartfelt clarinet playing sent "Ave Maria" wafting down from the choir loft. Second, I remember rejoicing with family at the reception as teen-age Cousin Danielle, who has Down's syndrome, exuberantly danced to the disco music with almost everyone else on the floor. Always, when I think of the wedding, I'll remember those stories and I'll smile.

But from this particular wedding, it is Nicole and Nikolaus who will have stories, first wedding stories and then marriage stories, as the days and years go by. Their stories will help sustain them and define who they are as individuals, as a couple, as God's own. We all have stories to remember and stories to tell, from our own lives. May they define and shape us toward God's will for us.

Thank You God for the stories of my life.

Printed in the United States
78167LV00001B/1-105